Be Free! The Gift of Freedom

Be Free! The Gift of Freedom

Where the Spirit of the Lord is, there is liberty.
2 Cor 3:17

Ricardo C. Castellanos
and
Allienne R. Becker

iUniverse, Inc.
New York Lincoln Shanghai

Be Free! The Gift of Freedom

iUniverse, Inc.

For information address:
iUniverse, Inc.
2021 Pine Lake Road, Suite 100
Lincoln, NE 68512
www.iuniverse.com

ISBN: 0-595-30539-3 (pbk)
ISBN: 0-595-66179-3 (cloth)

Printed in the United States of America

To True and Faithful Friends

Contents

Introduction

To be free is one of the profoundest desires of the human heart. Hoping to throw off all the constraints that bind us, we all long for freedom. Nowadays in our complex crowded society, we seem to keep losing more and more of our freedom. If we go to the library, our things have to be searched on the way out. We have to present a photo ID to travel on a plane. Before we get on the plane, we have to pass security, being asked even to take off our shoes to be sure we are not harboring a deadly weapon in them. Hidden cameras survey us as we walk the city streets. Everything we do is subject to scrutiny.

Everywhere fear haunts us. We are afraid of war, of terrorism, of new dreadful diseases that antibiotics cannot cure, among many other things. We fear what the future might bring. We fear suffering and pain, death and destruction. Our fears are endless. They are like chains that bind us, robbing us of our liberty.

Many of us are compulsive people. We cannot stop smoking, even when the medical establishment tells us that smoking kills. We overeat and consume too many alcoholic beverages. Young people become drug addicts. We are enslaved by our dependencies and desires.

Many of us refuse to accept reality and live as slaves to our fantasies. We try to manipulate and control those we love and take away their freedom. Searching for freedom in our possessions, we acquire more and more material things until we are bogged down in a mountain of things we hardly ever use.

We are enslaved by our passions that control us, instead of our controlling them. They are anger, lust, greed, envy, pride, gluttony, sloth or laziness. Any one of them can utterly bind us and destroy us.

Where do we look for freedom? Anyone who has ever studied philosophy knows that God is free. He is free always to do good, whereas we do things that we should not do, and leave undone the things we ought to do. St. Paul felt this very strongly. No doubt, we can all sympathize with him as he expresses his predicament:

> For the good that I will, I do not, but the evil which I will not, that I do. Now if I do that which I will not, it is no more I that do it, but sin that dwells in me. I find then a law, that when I have a will to do good, evil is present with

me. For I am delighted with the law of God, according to my members, fighting against the law of my mind, and captivating me in the law of sin, that is in my members. Unhappy man that I am, who shall deliver me from the body of this death? (Rom 7: 19–23)

St. Paul goes on to explain "with the mind, he serves the law of God, but with the flesh, the law of sin." Feeling this dichotomy within his being, he cries out, "Unhappy man that I am, who shall deliver me from the body of this death?" Immediately, he answers his own question. "The grace of God by Jesus Christ our Lord" (Rom 7: 25).

Our Lord Jesus Christ tells us that we are to seek the truth and it will set us free. In this book, we shall explore the various ways that Christ can set us free and what we have to do to find the freedom He promises in this life and in the life of the world to come.

Be Free from the Past

To be free, we must be reconciled with the past. Painful memories are like heavy chains binding many people to the past, haunting them relentlessly and giving them no peace. Many say they are weary, confounded, discouraged and find life not worth living. To them, to us all, Jesus calls: "Come unto me all you who labor, and are burdened, and I will refresh you. Take up my yoke upon you, and learn of me, because I am meek, and humble of heart; and you shall find rest to your souls" (Mt 11: 28–29). [1]

How do we find the rest that Jesus promises us? Before He will reveal His secrets to us, we must have the right attitudes. To enter His kingdom, we must become as little children (Mt 18: 3). The Holy Scripture tells us that God resists the proud and gives His grace to those who are humble (Jas 4: 6). So we must trust God and believe like little children do when their parents tell them something. The attitude of a Christian should be one of childlike acceptance.

Many who are especially troubled are so because events in their lives have not turned out well. In fact, many unfortunate things have happened to them and they feel rejected and defeated. They ask, "Why does God let bad things happen to us? This question is as old as the oldest book of the Bible—Job. When Job ponders the question of good and evil and seeks an answer from God, the Lord responds out of the whirlwind: "Who is this that darkens counsel with words without knowledge?" (Job 38: 2). After pointing out Job's ignorance to him, the Lord asks him "Where were you when I laid the foundations of the earth? Declare if you have understanding" (Job 38: 4). Finally God reminds Job: "All things that are under heaven are mine" (Job 41: 2). What He is saying is that since everything is His, He can do as wishes.

We simply do not know why bad things happen, but we do learn from Job and his experience that it is better not to ask God why. We simply accept that some things are inexplicable and that good and evil exist side by side. Sometimes it turns out that things we thought were good are disastrous and things we thought to be terrible, blessings.

When we adopt the attitude of a little child, we begin to understand. When the Lord promises to give us living water to drink, we don't ask Him where the water comes from or if it is hot or cold. We accept what He offers us and discover we have a marvelous blessing in our hearts.

Jesus calls all those who are seeking new strength and new possibilities to come to Him. He calls all who seek the truth and want to be free. He has what we have been looking for, but if we do not have childlike hearts, we will not understand that He is calling us. If we are proud and do not have hearts that are willing and eager to accept Him and His message, we will not understand what it is He wishes to do for us. Lacking understanding, we will not be able to find the rest He promises or the freedom we so desire.

Exactly what is the rest he offers us? Nothing less than refreshment and peace for our consciences, our minds, and our hearts. Many people are troubled with guilt all their lives, for we have all sinned and fallen short of the glory of God (Rom 3: 22–24). The Scripture tells us that even the just man may sin seven times a day. However, no matter what we have done or failed to do, we must remember that God loves us with the tender love of a mother for her newborn baby. He is the Good Shepherd who loves each of His sheep with an individual love and calls each one by name. He accepts us just as we are and blesses us.

Some people seem to feel they have to pay for their sins themselves. Even though they make a good sacramental confession of them, they continue to feel guilty. The Blood of Jesus shed on Calvary paid for every sin that has ever been committed or ever will be committed down until the end of time. In loving gratitude for Christ's atoning death on the cross, we must accept the satisfaction he has made for our sins and forgive ourselves. When we go to the Sacrament of Reconciliation, we receive the recitation of a prayer or other small action as a penance. However, these penances do not pay for our sins. We pray them as an act of thanksgiving that God has forgiven us. We accept His forgiveness that brings our hearts that are like spinning tops to tranquility and peace. As we receive his forgiveness, our consciences find rest and serenity and we are free from the burden of guilt that has been haunting us.

Many of us have experienced great disillusionment in our lives. Our friends, family members, and business associates have hurt us in many ways. Every day we continually experience things that give us pain and grieve us. God willingly, even eagerly, gives our hearts rest from these many wounds. Nevertheless, some people continue living in pain with aching hearts, not even wishing to communicate with other people at all, because of their brokenness.

People who are living in great pain because of their shattered lives are often belligerent and difficult to live with. Because they have been deeply hurt, they react by becoming very independent, ill tempered, basically anti-social and unable to trust anyone. This is not normal behavior, because everyone wishes to be loved, respected, and accepted.

In trying to help people who have been severely hurt, we have to trust God that He will protect us from their hateful behavior and that He will be our shield from their malevolence. The only hope for people who have been excessively injured is for them to learn to pardon all those who have ever offended them in any way. If they can truly forgive everyone, their hearts will find rest. If they do not, they will not see the glory of God.

What benefits are derived from pardoning people? Pardoning grants us inner peace and gives us the correct attitude toward others and ourselves. Some think that pardoning is difficult; actually, it is very easy. All we have to do is pray, observing the following three simple steps. We begin by confessing before God that we forgive those who have hurt us, even if we do not feel forgiveness in our hearts. There are three parts to our prayer of forgiveness. In the silence of our hearts we simply say: "Lord, pardon Joe; bless him; and bless me." When we see how simple this is to do, we wonder why we have put it off for so long.

Realizing that happiness comes from Jesus Christ, we put our confidence and trust in Him, for He will give rest not only to our souls and hearts, but physical rest as well. Not only will he give us rest, he will refresh us and give us new zest for living. In the book of Isaiah we read: "But they that wait upon the Lord shall renew their strength, they shall mount up with wings as eagles, they shall run, and not be weary, and they shall walk and not faint" (40: 31).

Let us look more closely now at those who have been deeply wounded in the course of their lives. Because they have been rebuffed and rejected, they may be completely desolate and miserable. They are often short tempered, annoyed, impatient, and bothered by everything that happens to them. Possessed of the wrong attitudes, they complain and groan about everything and everybody. Everyone, they think, mistreats them. Most of all, they are overcome by feelings of guilt. Obviously they need help. What can we do to help them? What can we do to help ourselves, if we have broken hearts and poor attitudes toward life? How can we break down the barriers that surround people in pain and deal effectively with their expressions of sadness, for such people almost invariably are victims of self-pity?

All attempts to bring healing to those who suffer from the wounds inflicted on them must begin with their examining their past lives to determine how they have hurt others. Acknowledging sins and confessing them to God and humbly and gratefully receiving His forgiveness must follow this. Unfortunately, some of us try to place our guilt on other people and deny our culpability.

We are all confronted by our problems and our sins. As rational people, we realize that we are responsible for all we do. We must not blame others for our failings. All our thoughts, desires, and decisions are ours. The problem arises that some people are not rational in that they regard their problems and sins emotionally, rather than rationally, which causes them to be very discouraged and deeply depressed.

In our country today, many people take medications to deal with chronic depression. Granted, some people are depressed because of chemical imbalances in their bodies; we are not trying to solve their problems, as medical doctors treat them. But normal people who suffer from depression are often so because of unpleasant events in their lives. Many hurtful memories have accumulated making them feel rejected, unwanted, and sour on life. A depressed person is a wounded person.

Some of those who have been broken from painful experiences become very aggressive, putting on an act of being strong and tough. Inside their hearts and souls, they are in a lamentable condition. Only by eliminating the roots of their bad humor and bitterness can they find peace and freedom from pain.

Still other people who have been broken by life act very proud. They too need to recognize that they need healing and transformation. The pain that is in their souls is like a cancer that insidiously grows until their entire life is dominated by it. They need a physician to heal the wounds of their hearts. The Scripture tells us that what comes out of the heart is what makes people impure. "There is nothing from without a man that entering into him, can defile him. But the things which come from a man, those are they that defile a man" (Mk 7:15).

The Divine Physician has the healing we all need for others and ourselves. In order to help these wounded people we have to forgive them completely just as God forgives them. We must absolve them from their hatred, resentment, and aggressiveness, while at the same time confronting all their hostility. We, and they, need to understand that the way to escape from feelings of hatred is by forgiving all those who have hurt us in any way. Forgiving and pardoning are the roads to spiritual peace and freedom.

We all must take ownership of all aspects of our lives. Everything within us is ours—our feelings, our desires, and our problems. External things are a different matter. It is extremely important to realize that we cannot control anyone else's actions. We have to let other people be free to be themselves. At most, we can venture an opinion from time to time, if one is requested.

Some people will treat us kindly, others indifferently, and still others will be malevolent towards us. For this reason, we have to adjust our expectations in regard to people. We need to be able to determine what we can expect from the various people in our lives, and not expect more than they are willing to give.

Some people like to regard themselves as victims, but we are not victims of anyone—not of our spouses, our parents, our children, or our friends. Every time an adult individual is victimized without a physical or moral gun pointing at her/him is because s/he has chosen to allow others to be victimizers. We are free agents and must let other people be likewise free.

So how are we to deal with the people who are broken by life and have not yet found freedom in Christ? By praying for them, blessing them, and most importantly knowing when to be silent.

To find freedom from the past we need to learn to smile at life, receive the Holy Spirit into our hearts, and begin living a life of forgiveness, reconciliation, and peace. Jesus Christ is the only Savior and He is the same today as He was yesterday and will be forever. He has the power to bring us joy today by healing our hearts, giving us the ability to be reconciled with everyone.

"Lord, we accept Your gift of freedom from the past, by letting you take away all our sins and healing our memories of them. We forgive everyone that has ever harmed us, and pray that they will also forgive us for our offenses against them. Help us to live better lives starting right now. Our hearts are open to receiving Your light and guidance; fill them with love for You and for all who have ever harmed us in any way. We thank You that we are now free from the past and ready to begin new lives in Your love. Amen."

Freedom from Darkness

Breaking free from the past is just the first step in obtaining total spiritual freedom. Once we are free from haunting memories and guilt, we need to emerge from the darkness that has bound us and enter into the light. Jesus tells us that He has come into the world as a light so that anyone who believes in Him will not remain in darkness (Jn 12: 46).

To escape from the darkness that obscures our vision, we have to make an act of the will determining to enter into the light. Some people are lost in spiritual blackness, making no attempt to escape, probably not realizing that it is even possible to do so. Perhaps they are following blind guides who are unable to lead them to the light.

Far worse than those who are lost in darkness are those among us who deliberately refuse to follow the light, and live embracing obscurity, confusion, and madness, suffering from all kinds of problems and difficulties with their bodies sick and dying because of the choices they make to indulge in things that are harmful and destructive. Illness contributes to increasing and strengthening all the self-destructive elements within us. We succumb to disease because of the devastation caused by living in darkness, opting for the wrong choices. To heal our minds, souls, and bodies, we must change our attitudes.

Family life is in chaos, because we choose to neglect our families and pursue courses that lead to divorce and the break up of the family. Feeling sorry for ourselves, we turn to all kinds of painkillers to ease the torment we feel in the darkness of our minds and souls. Self-pity consumes us, as we feel unloved and unwanted.

We encounter great emptiness in our lives, suffering because we value transient things that are material and do not contribute to our spiritual welfare or happiness. The problem is not new. For centuries people have been experiencing the spiritual darkness that comes with seeking for happiness where it cannot be found. "'Vanity of vanities,' said Ecclesiastes, 'vanity of vanities, and all is vanity'" (Ecc 1: 2). The Biblical author continues by explaining what he means:

And when I turned myself to all the works which my hands had wrought, and to the labors wherein I had labored in vain, I saw in all things vanity, and vexation of mind, and that nothing was lasting under the sun. (Ecc 2: 11)

And therefore I was weary of my life, when I saw that all things under the sun are evil, and all vanity and vexation of spirit. (Ecc 2: 17)

The vacuity of material and transient things is the ever-recurrent theme of the book of Ecclesiastes, stressing that we are never satisfied. Nothing we hear, see, do, or possess satisfies us for long. We are incapable of being satisfied. What is more, our culture foments our dissatisfaction by constantly urging us to purchase new cars, fashions, and electronic gadgetry. We are encouraged to believe that when we buy all these new things that we will be happy. At best they provide a little transient pleasure.

Speaking for God, the prophet Isaiah, calls out to all those who are convinced of the vain emptiness of all life apart from God.

All you that thirst come to the waters, and you that have no money make haste, buy, and eat. Come, buy wine and milk without money, and without any price. Why do you spend money for that which is not bread, and you labor for that which does not satisfy you? Hearken diligently to me, and eat that which is good, and your soul shall be delighted in fatness. Incline your ear and come to me. Hear and your soul shall live, and I will make an everlasting covenant with you, the faithful mercies of David. (Is 55: 1–3)

Loose the bands of wickedness, undo the bundles that oppress, let them that are broken go free, and break asunder every burden. (Is 58: 6)

Isaiah directs us in the response we are to make to God's call: "Seek the Lord, while he may be found: call upon Him, while He is near" (Is 58: 6). God will set us free from all slavery and give us happiness. When we find happiness in Him, sadness, infirmity, and addiction will no longer enslave us.

Come let us drink of the Water of Life and eat the Living Bread that comes down from heaven. We will find joy in Jesus Christ who will give us a reason to live and a reason to die, when the time comes. The word of God never returns empty to Him, but does what it is intended to do (Is 55: 11). It is an effective, transforming word that can change our lives forever and it will make it possible for us to confront any situation. Most importantly, it will take us out of the darkness into the light. Christ will heal all the wounds that we have received in the past and bring us to spiritual health. Let us trust the Holy Scripture when it tells us: "He was wounded for our iniquities, He was bruised for our sins. The chastisement of our peace was upon Him, and by His bruises we are healed" (Is 53: 5).

As God heals and transforms us, we will learn that purchasing things is a means, not an end in itself. We cannot live without money, food, clothing, and cars, among other things, but when we have found the freedom God gives, we will no longer put our heart into these things that give us only interior emptiness. With the Samaritan woman who encountered Jesus at Jacob's well, we will ask Him to give us His living water so that we will no longer thirst. We will partake of His Living Bread that comes down from heaven so that His life will dwell in us, knowing that in so doing that He will raise us up on the last day to eternal life.

Jesus comes to us, asking us to give Him a little of our time. Although he is all-powerful, he needs us to give him our time, hearts, and lives. Only He can give us interior peace, freedom, and escape from the darkness. Once we have experienced His light, we can say with St. Paul: "For God, who commanded the light to shine out of darkness, has shined in our hearts, to give the light of the knowledge of the glory of God, in the face of Christ Jesus" (2 Cor 4: 6). Hitherto we were in darkness, but now we walk as children of the light (Eph 5: 11).

One of the best indications that we are now in the light is that we love our brothers and sisters in Christ. St. John makes this very clear: "But he that hates his brother, is in darkness, and walks in darkness, and knows not where he goes, because the darkness has blinded his eyes" (1 Jn 2: 11). St. Matthew explains that our eyes are the light of our bodies, and if our eyes are evil our whole body shall be dark and our darkness shall be very great indeed (Mt 6: 23).

Some of us have tremendous wounds to be healed and do not even realize how serious they are. We suffer from unjustifiable anger, non-clinical depression, and irrational fears, to name a few of the things that plague us. As we seek healing for them, let us ask the Lord to balance our emotions and feelings. Living on an emotional roller coaster as some people do is undesirable. Serenity is needed in our emotional lives and is a gift for which we need to pray. We also need to feed our minds, hearts, and souls with the Word of God. We must know what His word says, if it is to be a transforming force in our lives. The thoughts and attitudes that we learn from God in reading His Word will change our thoughts. As we change our ways of thinking, our hearts will be transformed and we will begin to live our new lives in Christ with His Word directing and guiding us. As our lives change, we will discover that we are no longer confessing the same sins year after year, but we will be making progress in attaining the liberty of the children of God.

"Lord, we lift our hearts up to you, believing that with one word You can heal us and take away our darkness. We want to walk in the light with You. We ask you to give us serenity in our emotional lives and heal our bodies so that we may serve You. Give us light to guide us on our way to freedom in You. Help us to understand that our happiness is to be found only in You and not in our material possessions. We know that You are light and in You there is no darkness. We want to be like You; fill us with Your light so that we may shine as lights in the darkness of the world. Amen."

Jesus Sets Us Free

The names Holy Scripture gives to Jesus tell us very much about Him and give us insights that help us to know Him better. Names in almost every language have a meaning, although the meaning is often forgotten. Originally the name of a person was meant to reflect his/her predominant characteristic or a quality the parents wished the child to have when they named it. In this chapter we are considering some of the names given to Jesus in the Bible so we will know Him better.

Jesus tells us He is the TRUTH (Jn 14: 16). Let's listen to His words:

> And you shall know the truth, and the truth shall make you free. They answered him: "We are the seed of Abraham, and we have never been slaves to any man. How do you say, you shall be free?" Jesus answered them: "Amen, amen I say unto you, that whosoever commits sin, is the servant of sin. Now the servant abides not in the house forever, but the son abides forever. If therefore the son shall make you free, you shall be free indeed." (Jn 8: 34–36)

Jesus tells us that He is truth and if we seek Him, He will make us free and if He sets us free we shall be free indeed. What a wonderful promise! And what fulfillment! When the truth governs us, we have nothing to fear, because the truth sets things right and deepens human relationships. Truth stands for faithfulness and Jesus tells us that He is faithful.

One of the names for Jesus found in the book of Revelation, also known as the Apocalypse of St. John from its Greek title, is "ALPHA AND OMEGA." At the beginning of this awesome book we read: "I am Alpha and Omega, the beginning and the end, says the Lord God, who is, and who was, and who is to come, the Almighty" (Rev 1: 8). After saying this, the Lord directs John to write down all that he will see and send it to the churches. Since this revelation is to be derived from a vision and written down, it differs from the prophecies of the Old Testament prophets that are received and promulgated orally. John's writing is called an apocalypse. In time the word "apocalypse" came to refer to any spiritual event that speaks of the end of the world.

Again in Revelation 21: 6, the Lord speaks to John: "It has already happened. I am the Alpha and the Omega, the Beginning and the End. I will give water from the well of life freely to anybody who is thirsty." And then for a third time the title Alpha and Omega is employed to refer to Jesus (Rev. 22: 13).

There are great similarities between the title of Alpha and Omega applied to Christ and descriptions of Yahweh in the Book of Isaiah. In Isaiah we read: "Who has worked and done these things, calling the generations from the beginning? I the Lord, I am the first and the last." Later in the book of Isaiah, we read: "Thus says the Lord, the King of Israel, and His Redeemer the Lord of Hosts: I am the first, and I am the last, and besides me there is no God" (Is 44: 6). And again for a third time, paralleling the triple usage in Revelation: "Hearken to me, O Jacob, and you Israel whom I call. I am He, I am the first, and I am the last. My hand also has founded the earth, and my right hand has measured the heavens. I shall call them, and they shall stand together" (Is 48: 12–13).

The alpha and the omega are the first and the last letters of the Greek alphabet, however, the author who is writing in Greek and referring to the Greek letters probably has in mind the way people from the Hebrew culture employed the first and last letters of the Hebrew alphabet to indicate the entirety of the Lord's presence in human history from the creation of the world until the end of time. By paralleling the language of Isaiah speaking of Yahweh, the reader knows the author is identifying the Alpha and Omega, Jesus Christ, with Yahweh, the Ancient of Days, of the Hebrew people in order to emphasize the divinity of Christ and His oneness with the Father. To St. John, Jesus is the Lord of Time who holds the past, present, and future in His hands.

Time is the most impacting reality in our lives. We are born at a particular moment in time and we die at a particular time. There is absolutely nothing we can do to escape time, as it flies inexorably by, taking us from the cradle to the grave. But what is time? We find it difficult to describe. We feel its effects, but are hard pressed to explain what it is. What does the *American Heritage Dictionary* have to tell us? It is "a non spatial continuum in which events occur in apparently irreversible order from past to present and future" This definition does not really add much to our understanding of the concept of time.

We realize that we view time subjectively, because sometimes events seem to transpire very slowly, such as when we are in pain. On the other hand, time seems to race by when we are enjoying life. Time is a gift from God and although we all receive the same twenty-four hours a day, some of us seem to accomplish more in a day than others. Life spans vary in length, so that some have many more days than others and are able to accomplish far more. Time is also a mystery, because we do not know what the morrow will bring. However, knowing that Christ, the Alpha and the Omega and the Lord of Time, holds the past, present, and the future in His hands gives us peace. Since He lives outside of time, He perceives everything that happens in time as occurring simultaneously. Our whole existence is in His hands—all that we have and all that we are and everything else that exists—all is in the hands of our glorious Redeemer. We do not have to be concerned about the past, because He forgives us all our sins and makes up for our failings. He is always with us at the present moment guiding and directing us. We do not have to worry about the future, because He lives in our future. Since He dwells in light inaccessible outside the bounds of time, He sees everything as happening in an Eternal Now. Everything is present to Him. In fact, He already sees us glorified in heaven with Him. We do not have to worry about our health, what will become of us, or even how to pay our bills, because the future is in His hands. As St. Paul assures us: "We know that to them that love God, all things work together unto good, to such as, according to his purpose, are called to be saints" (Rom 8: 28).

Another title given to the Savior is the GREAT AMEN. We find this in the following verse of Scripture: "And to the angel of the church of Laodicea, write: These things says the Amen, the faithful and true witness, who is the beginning of the creation of God" (Rev 3: 14). Jesus is given this title because He establishes God's purposes on earth. In effect, he says "Amen" to whatever the Father proposes with His "amen" signifying, "Yes, I agree, may it happen!" Jesus is the great amen to the will of the Heavenly Father, fulfilling His plan for humanity. He is the incarnation of the Word of God and also the great amen to our lives, because He says amen to our being alive and continuing to live. Let us enjoy all the wonderful things He has given us—our health, family, friends, because Jesus says "amen" to our lives.

How beautiful and inspiring to know that God has and continues to have faith in us. We believe in God, but do we realize that He also believes in us? It is something to consider. Because He also believes in us, He gives us grace and the sacraments and we become His children as we are born to new life in the baptismal font of the Church. He believes that we have the capability of becoming His children, by receiving His Word and by believing in Him. He believes we can be good people who are able to love and to forgive. How wonderful it is to know that He has faith in us and truly believes in us, in spite of all our failings, defects, weaknesses, and sins. Understanding this helps us to do all that He expects of us. God, the Father, whose love for us is everlasting, also hopes in us that we will become better people.

Every moment of our lives when we respond affirmatively and positively to God, Jesus says, "Amen." When we praise God, love him, have faith and hope in Him, Jesus says, "Amen." When, during the liturgy, we say, "Amen," Jesus also says, "Amen."

In prayer, what is most important is not what we say, but what God says.

In speaking of prayer, John Paul II writes the following that explains the importance of Gods participation in our prayer:

> *In prayer then, the true protagonist is God.* The protagonist is Christ, who constantly frees creation from slavery to corruption and leads it toward liberty, for the glory of the children of God. The protagonist is the *Holy Spirit*, who "comes to the aid of our weakness." We begin to pray, believing that it is our initiative that compels us to do so. Instead, we learn that it is always God's initiative within us, just as St. Paul has written. *This initiative restores in us our true humanity; it restores in us our unique dignity.* Yes, we are brought into the higher dignity of the children of God, who are the hope of all creation. (*Threshold* 17)

God is always the one who speaks first in our prayer. Sooner than we realize, He is with us. Not just a transcendental being who hung the stars in the heavens and carved out the depths of the seas and the hollows of the land, He is a God who draws near.

He comes so close to us that He wants us to regard him as a friend. The name of FRIEND is one that we greatly cherish when we apply it to Jesus. Here is what He says to us: "I will not now call you servants, for the servant does not know what his lord is doing. But I have called you friends, because all things whatsoever I have heard of my Father, I have made known to you (Jn 15:15).

How wonderful it is that we are not servants, but rather the beloved of His heart and we are able to establish an intimate and personal relationship of friendship and love with Him.

We all have friends, but only one Divine Friend—Jesus Christ, the friend that has promised never to leave us or abandon us. We read in the media of family members who donate a kidney to save a brother or sister. Some give even one of their eyes to help someone who cannot see. Other people give their fortunes to benefit people in need, such as the recently canonized Mother Katherine Drexel (1858–1966) who inherited an investment banking fortune worth fourteen million dollars and used her entire fortune to teach black and Native American children and found the Sisters of the Blessed Sacrament to carry out her mission. These acts of charity are wonderful, but cannot compare with what our Divine

Friend Jesus has done for us. So that we would have eternal life, He gave every drop of His precious Blood. What is more, He promises us health, prosperity, and love and an eternity to enjoy them. We have forever to love and be loved. This is eternal life—we are already in it. The Holy Scripture tells us plainly: "Now this is eternal life: That they may know You, the only true God, and Jesus Christ, whom You have sent"(Jn 17: 3). If we know Him, we are *already* in eternal life. Jesus Himself tells us that if we eat His flesh and drink His blood we shall never die. "And everyone that lives, and believes in me, shall not die forever" (Jn 11: 26). We will walk though the valley of the shadow of death, but a shadow cannot harm us. The shadow of death will flee when Christ the Light of the World shall dissipate all shadows and bring us into the brightness of eternal day.

He has blessed us beyond what we ever could have dreamed possible, revealing to us all that His Father has revealed to Him. Wishing to be in union with us, he laid down life for us, his friends. No greater love is there than that.

Friendship with Jesus Christ, based on interpersonal knowledge, is something very special and unique. The most important thing in our relationship with Christ is to augment the profundity of the friendship we enjoy with Him. We do this by getting to know Him better. The more people know each other as they really are, the deeper the friendship becomes.

In the same way knowing Christ brings us closer to Him. The way actually to know Him is through His Word, His Church, and His sacraments, for they will all bring us into intimate union with Him. Once we get to know Him in this way, He will no longer be a stranger, but our best friend whom we address in terms of endearment.

As we draw closer to Jesus and grow in His friendship, we find that we begin to love Him more and more and detest sin. The Holy Scripture tells us: "And by this we know that we have known Him, if we keep His commandments" (1 Jn 2: 3). Sometimes unfortunately, however, God's children do fall into sin. John hastens to explain: "But if any man sin, we have an advocate with the Father, Jesus Christ, the just, and He is the propitiation for our sins: and not for ours only, but also for those of the whole world" (1 Jn 2: 1–2).

ADVOCATE is another of the names given to Jesus and one we treasure very highly. If we sin, Jesus is just, but how wonderful it is to know He is our advocate before the throne of His Father pleading our case, saying: "Don't look at their sins, look instead at my blood which I shed for them." There is not a better advocate in the tribunal of the Father. In this litigious country, how wonderful it is to know that we have an advocate who will defend us in any court.

When people ask us for the name of a lawyer, we always recommend Jesus Christ, our defender and advocate in heaven and on earth. We tell people who are facing divorce, "Get Jesus Christ for your lawyer. He won't get you a divorce, but He will repair your marriage." Who can destroy us when we have Jesus Christ for all the cases of our life? Who can condemn us, when Jesus pleads our case? Moreover, he will not destroy our friends; he will convert them. Most importantly, he will set us free, as He promises—free from the chains that bind us.

Perhaps the favorite title that most people have for Jesus is one He applied to Himself when He said "I am the Good Shepherd" (Jn 10:11). The people of the Bible have always looked to Yahweh as their shepherd and speaking through the prophet Ezekiel, He refers to Himself in this way. "For thus says the Lord God: Behold I myself will seek my sheep, and will visit them" (Ez 34: 11).

We identify the GOOD SHEPHERD with the psalm of David stating that the Lord is my shepherd. The psalmist expresses his profound trust in the Shepherd saying that he shall lack nothing, that the shepherd provides for all his needs, by leading him into green pastures by the still waters where He refreshes his soul. The comparison of Jesus to a shepherd demonstrates His loving care for us. In the days of both the Old and New Testaments, a shepherd rose early in the morning to begin caring for his sheep. He would take them from the fold where they spent the night and lead them to the pastures where they were to spend the day. If one of them strayed, he sought it out and brought it back to be with the others. Water has always been scarce in the land of the Bible and it was the shepherd's duty to provide water for his flock. At the end of the day, he brought them back to the fold where one by one they walked under his staff as he counted them to be sure all were safely in the fold.

The psalmist says that he has no fear because the Lord, as shepherd, protects him and guides him. He also anoints his head with oil to drive away the pesky insects that pester the sheep. If wild animals attack the sheep under the darkness of night, he drives them off. Jesus is our Good Shepherd. As a faithful shepherd He never leaves us or abandons us in times of trial. He refreshes us with the Water of Life, the gift of the Holy Spirit, and nourishes us with the Living Bread that comes down from heaven. He defends us from all our enemies and leads us and guides us into His eternal kingdom and the glorious freedom of the children of God.

The WORD OF GOD is one of the most frequently used titles for Jesus Christ. At the beginning of St. John's Gospel, Christ is referred to as the Word and identified with God. John tells us that, "In the beginning was the Word, and the Word was with God, and the Word was God. The same was in the beginning with God. All things were made by Him: and without Him was made nothing that was made" (Jn 1: 1–3). Leaving absolutely no question about the divinity of Christ Jesus, John writes :

> He was in the world, and the world was made by Him, and the world knew Him not. He came unto his own, and His own received Him not. But as many as received Him, He gave them power to be made the sons of God, to them that believe in His name. Who are born, not of blood, nor of the will of the flesh, nor of the will of man, but of God. And the Word was made flesh, and dwelt among us, (and we saw His glory, the glory as it were of the only begotten of the Father,) full of grace and truth. (Jn 1: 10–14)

Surely one of the most beautiful passages in all of Scripture, theses few sentences make it very clear that Jesus is God and that He gives men and women power to become sons and daughters of the eternal Father.

The title Word of God is also applied to Jesus in the book of Revelation that has also traditionally been attributed to the authorship of the Apostle John. Whether he actually wrote it or not, we cannot be sure. However, it was no doubt inspired by his thought and it can be definitely said that its inspiration was Johannine. In his apocalyptic vision, the author beholds a magnificent and glorious portrait of our Lord Jesus Christ. Consider it:

> And I saw heaven opened, and behold a white horse; and He that sat upon him was called faithful and true, and with justice doth He judge and fight. And His eyes were as a flame of fire, and on His head were many diadems, and He had a name written, which no man knows but Himself. And He was clothed with a garment sprinkled with blood; and His name is called, THE WORD OF GOD. And the armies that are in heaven followed Him on white horses, clothed in fine linen, white and clean. And out of His mouth proceeds a sharp two-edged sword, that with it He may strike the nations. And He shall rule them with a rod of iron, and He treads the winepress of the fierceness of the wrath of God the Almighty and He hath on His garment, and on His thigh written: KING OF KINGS, AND LORD OF LORDS. And I saw an angel standing in the sun, and he cried with a loud voice, saying to all the birds that did fly through the midst of heaven: Come, gather yourselves together to the great supper of God." (Rev 19: 11–18)

In this eschatological vision, Christ is seen in all His power ready to bring justice to the nations. No longer is He the suffering servant, but now the King of Kings, and the Lord of Lords, two titles that reflect His majesty, grandeur, and splendor.

Also in the book of Revelation we find Christ referred to as the LAMB OF GOD who is described as slain (Rev 5: 6). In the vision, thousands upon thousands are gathered about the throne, saying: "The Lamb that was slain is worthy to receive power, and divinity, and wisdom, and strength, and honor, and glory, and benediction" (Rev 5: 12). A great multitude of people from all nations, tribes, and peoples are standing before the throne wearing white robes and carrying palm branches in their hands, crying out: "Salvation to our God, who sits upon the throne, and to the Lamb" (7: 9–10). They are God's faithful elect and have washed their robes in the blood of the Lamb, the King of Kings and the Lord of Lords, and made them white. All the angels and many others fall upon their faces and adore God, saying: "Amen. Benediction, and glory, and wisdom, and thanksgiving, honor, and power, and strength to our God forever and ever. Amen" (7: 11).

Later we are told: "Let us be glad and rejoice, and give glory to Him; for the marriage of the Lamb is come, and His wife has prepared herself. And it is granted to her that she should clothe herself with fine linen, glittering and white. For the fine linen are the justifications of saints" (19: 7–8). The Bride of the Lamb of God, Jesus Christ, is the Church. We too shall be in that group, if we are faithful and true and persevere in patience. This depiction of the Lamb of God and the worship that the blessed give Him is especially beautiful and inspiring and should encourage us to victory in our daily struggles.

In the book of Revelation, Jesus refers to himself saying, "I am the MORNING STAR" (Rev 22: 16). "I, Jesus, have sent my angel, to testify to you these things in the churches. I am the root and stock of David, the bright and morning star." The Apostle Peter also refers to Jesus as the day star when he says, "And we have the more firm prophetical word: where unto you do well to attend, as to a light that shines in a dark place, until the day dawn, and the day star arise in your hearts" (2 Pe 1: 19). What is alluded to by calling Christ the Morning or Day Star is that He is the light of the world that the darkness can never extinguish. It also means that Jesus is the beginning of the dawn of a new era when He will finally reign and when His light will completely illuminate His followers. In Rev 2: 28 Jesus promises to give the Morning Star to those who are triumphant in the battle with the world, the flesh, and the devil. He will give Himself to all who overcome, filling them to overflowing with His light and joy.

"Lord, we seek the Truth, we seek You. Give us the freedom you have promised to those whose hearts are set on you. You are the Alpha and Omega of our lives. You have accompanied us every step we have taken from our mothers' arms. What a friend You are! May we always live for Your friendship. You are our advocate who never fails us, our Good Shepherd who laid down His life that we might live, nevermore to die. You are the Word of God that enlightens our minds and hearts, the Lamb that was slain for us. You are the Morning Star that shines into the darkness of this world and is a lamp unto our feet on the paths of righteousness. Lead us into the eternal kingdom of Your light and glory. Give us the liberty of the children of God. Amen."

Freedom to Pray

We seek freedom but often look for it in the wrong places. We do not encounter liberty, as many assume, in doing everything we want to do. Rather liberty is doing what is good and what fulfills us. True liberty helps us to attain the most important things in life—self-realization, peace, and joy. We can only find true liberty in Jesus Christ. A very important inward and outward reality, freedom is His gift to those who seek Him. We cannot find true liberty in pleasure that might brighten a few hours, but cannot provide lasting freedom and the peace and joy that accompany it.

Many people think that liberty consists in the intellectual and physical ability to choose to think or move as one pleases. They identify freedom with liberal thought. To understand intellectual freedom it is necessary first to comprehend spiritual freedom.

A person can be intellectually free and spiritually bound. In this country with its great traditions of freedom, we have the most depressed people in the world. Many suffer from loneliness. We kill more unborn babies than all the people the Nazis killed in their concentration camps.

Spiritual liberty is the first and primary liberty that we need to attain in our search for freedom, because it makes it possible for us to be mentally and physically free. Being physically free means enjoying things that are beneficial for our bodies. On the contrary, misusing food, alcohol, and drugs will bring us sickness and destruction.

How do we attain to spiritual liberty? It only comes from Jesus Christ who grants us His grace to be able to do what is best for us and fills us with His peace so that our hearts overflow with joy. Liberty consists in knowing the love of God and realizing that everything aside from His love takes our freedom away.

The free heart is the one that knows Jesus Christ has given it liberty and life. Everything we have is a gift from Him. The one who seeks freedom and peace, and finds it, is the person that says, "Thank you, Lord, that You love me so much that You have pardoned me of all the things that I have done wrong." Having said this, we should break into praise to show our gratitude to God for forgiving us and blessing us with everything we are and have. Our hearts should explode in praise. We should imitate Mary, the Mother of Beautiful Love, whose praise burst forth in the canticle known as the *Magnificat*. "My soul magnifies the Lord and my spirit rejoices in God my Savior." This is the beginning of liberty. Praise is a sign of liberty.

The first step toward this level of intellectual and physical liberty in our lives is found in loving Jesus Christ and letting His love cause our hearts to explode in praise. Doing this, we begin to feel free and with Mary give thanks to the Lord that He has done such wonderful things in us. Our hearts are grateful and we rejoice in living. We praise Him and thank Him for having given us life in such abundance. We rejoice and praise Him that we are alive, that we can see the beautiful world He has created, that we can love and be loved. Praise is the response of a heart that is free, manifesting our love for God. Praise also converts us into living sacrifices—oblations. St. Paul urges us make oblations of ourselves:

> I beseech you therefore, brethren, by the mercy of God, that you present your bodies a living sacrifice, holy, pleasing unto God, your reasonable service. And be not conformed to this world, but be reformed in the newness of your mind, that you may prove what is the good, and the acceptable, and the perfect will of God. (Rom 12: 1–2)

When our minds are renewed in this fashion, we can better understand what God wants of us and how He will lead us into freedom. He has called us out of the darkness to announce His praise. We are "a chosen nation, a purchased people" that we may praise Him (1Pet 2: 9). The very purpose of our lives is to praise God. When we do, our praise does not make Him greater. We cannot add anything to Him. Our hearts are enlarged in praising Him. We are called to praise Him and be grateful for all His blessings. We are blessed even more when we proclaim and announce the greatness of our God and all His marvels.

Praising God and loving Him makes our hearts sing with joy. We let our love flow from our hearts saying: "How much we love you, Lord, our Savior. How wonderful it is to be with You, Lord! We bless you; we praise you; we glorify you; we give You thanks for Your great glory!"

Our hearts are bigger now that we have been praising Him. Now we are free to love His Word, His sacraments, and His Church. There is also more room in them for loving everyone. There is enough room in our hearts that we can embrace the whole world, with praise giving us the right attitudes towards God and man.

We recognize that God is supreme and that our praise has increased our love for Him. We accept His Word as absolute truth with an expectant faith that will enable us to encounter all difficulties and problems that we face. We all must realize our mortality; all cures on earth are but temporal, but when we enter into the brightness of Eternal Day we will all be young again.

Everywhere we meet people who are afflicted and have serious problems. Some are suffering from dread diseases. Others have family problems and are facing divorce. With our hearts filled with compassion we say to all: "Praise the Lord!" In praising the Lord, we will find freedom, peace, and joy even in the midst of the trials of this life.

The Lord has loved us from all eternity. Let us tell Him that we are not coming to Him in prayer to ask for favors, but just to praise Him for the rest of our lives. We are people of praise. Let us wake in the morning singing with joy, for a heart that sings is a happy heart.

Many people who sit in the pews of a church do not like to sing. Perhaps it is because they do not feel they have a reason to sing. Perhaps they do not realize the wonderful things God has done for them. We need to sing God's praises, for in so doing we are transformed. When we hear a congregation sing the praises of God with great enthusiasm and verve, we know they have a special love for Christ.

St. Paul tells us that we are to speak to ourselves in "psalms, and hymns, and spiritual canticles, singing and making melody" in our hearts to the Lord (Eph 5: 19). In short, we are to be enthusiastic in our prayer.

After we have become accustomed to singing the praises of God, we begin clapping our hands in response to His presence in our midst as we worship Him in corporate praise. We need to let the Lord free us to express our love and praise in this way. After all, in St. Peter's in Rome, people applaud the presence of the Holy Father. Why shouldn't we applaud the presence of the Lord?

The next step in finding liberty in worship is lifting our hands in prayer.

This is a good Biblical tradition recommended by St. Paul in his first letter to Timothy. "I will therefore that men pray in every place, lifting up pure hands, without anger and contention" (1 Ti 2: 8).

With our hands lifted up we begin to release the deepest feelings of our hearts. We talk to God as our Father, letting our love flow from our hearts to His heart. We lift our hands and arms like little children do when they want their Father to pick them up, embrace them, and carry them. We want Him to surround us with all His glory and give us total security as He embraces us.

As we draw nearer to God, we experience greater freedom. Rejoicing in the Lord we celebrate, much as people in the world do, but we have no need for any intoxicating beverages, for the Holy Spirit is the only intoxicant we ever need.

To get some idea of how Christian people can celebrate, we will look at a great celebration the people of Israel had upon the return from their time of captivity in Babylon. When the people were settled in their homes, Esdras, or Ezra, read the Law of Moses to the people, explaining to them how they were to celebrate the feast of tabernacles

> And Esdras opened the book before all the people, for he was above all the people, and when he had opened it, all the people stood. And Esdras blessed the Lord, the great God, and all the people answered, amen, amen, lifting up their hands and they bowed down, and adored God with their faces to the ground. (Neh 8: 5–6)

Interestingly Eastern Orthodox Christians still bow down and adore God with their faces to the ground as a regular part of the celebration of the Divine Liturgy of St. John Chrysostom. Also like the Israelites mentioned above, they stand to worship God, except when they make their profound bows of adoration.

A few days later the people of Israel gathered to fast in order to show sorrow for their sins. The Levites called them to prayer:

> Arise, bless the Lord your God from eternity to eternity, and blessed be the high name of Your glory with all blessing and praise. You, Yourself, O Lord alone, You have made heaven and the heaven of heavens, and all the host thereof, the earth and all things that are in it, the seas and all that are therein, and You give life to all these things, and the host of heaven adores You. (Neh 9: 6–7)

The people then prayed with great devotion confessing their sins. A short time later, they had the dedication of the wall of the city of Jerusalem that they had rebuilt, celebrating with processions on the wall. Some blew trumpets; other played on harps like King David had. Singers sang at the top of their voices. In their celebration of gratitude and praise, they made so much noise that it could be heard miles away (Neh 12: 43).

Today we see people celebrate relatively insignificant things and become excessively jubilant. On television people scream with delight when they win a little money on a quiz show. Other people yell expressing their enthusiasm at football games. Why should not Christians shout when Jesus lifts them up out of difficulties?

Having reached this stage of liberty in prayer, people shout, "Alleluia!" or "Glory to God!" When our hearts are enflamed with great love for God, they pour forth correspondingly great praise. If we turn now to the psalms, we will find a wealth of praise to use in our adoration. Here are a few examples:

> O Lord, how admirable is your name in the whole earth! For Your magnificence is elevated about the heavens. (Ps 8: 2)

> I will give praise to You, O Lord, with my whole heart; I will relate all your wonders. I will be glad and rejoice in you. I will sing to Your name, O You most high. (Ps 9: 2–3)

> I will extol You, O Lord, for You have upheld me and have not made my enemies to rejoice over me. O Lord, my God, I have cried to You and You have healed me. (Ps 29: 2–3)

We sing God's praises with our lips, our hearts, and our understanding. If our hearts are willing to grow into a deeper stage of prayer, God may provide us with a prayer language for the times when we simply run out of words. We just let the words rise up inside our hearts and then try sounding them out. Perhaps it will sound like gibberish to us, but the Holy Scripture tells us that the Spirit prays in us. "For we know not what we should pray for as we ought, but the Spirit itself makes intercession for us with groanings which cannot be uttered" (Rom: 8: 26). So let us be free in the liberty of the Spirit, letting Him guide our prayer.

As we keep growing in freedom in prayer, the next thing we can do is compose our own song to sing to the Lord. The Scripture itself suggests we do this. "Give praise to the Lord on the harp; sing to him with the psaltery, the instrument of ten strings. Sing unto Him a new canticle, sing well unto Him with a loud noise" (Ps 32: 2–3).

The Israelites made it a practice to compose new songs or canticles to the Lord for special occasions. Mary sang to Him her *Magnificat* at the annunciation when the Angel Gabriel told her she was to be the mother of the Messiah. In some points, it resembles Hannah's song of praise that she sang after Samuel was born, but Mary's version is much longer and more complete (Is 2: 1).

Our songs to the Lord do not have to be elaborate; they must be heartfelt. It is truly beautiful when we compose our own songs for the Lord. In them, we can use the names of endearment that we love best in approaching Him. The Scripture tells us that the Lord also has a special name for each of us. "To him that overcomes, I will give to eat of the hidden manna and will give him a white stone and in the stone a new name written, which no man knows saving he that receives it" (Rev 2: 17). Perhaps it might be interesting to wonder what the names are the Lord has selected for each of us. In composing our songs of praise to the Lord we can enumerate the marvels of God and all the wonderful things He has done for us.

Anyone wanting to advance in liberating prayer should next consider adding dance to his worship. This is sound Biblical practice. Here is what the Scripture tells us about King David.

> So David went, and brought away the ark of God out of the house of Obededom into the city of David with joy. And there were with David seven choirs, and calves for victims. And when they that carried the ark of the Lord had gone six paces, he sacrificed an ox and a ram. And David danced with all his might before the Lord, and David was girded with a linen ephod. And David and all the house of Israel brought the Ark of the Covenant of the Lord with joyful shouting, and with the sound of trumpets. (2 Sa 6: 12)

When we add dancing to our worship in addition to our singing, we are responding totally to the love of God. When we make a total response like this to God, wonderful things will begin to happen in our lives. Let us praise God with hymns. Let us dance for joy in His presence. What a wonderful freedom of worship we offer Him! How truly liberated we feel.

"Lord, teach us to worship you in beauty and in truth. Make our hearts your tabernacles in this world. Fill us with your presence. Let your joy transform us and make us completely yours. We thank you that we are called to be a people of praise. Teach us to praise you as befits your glory. We thank you for the beautiful universe that speaks so poignantly of You. We thank You for Your love that transforms us and draws us to You. Unite us to you that we may always do Your will. Make us like Jesus, in whose name we pray, so that we may serve You for ever and ever. Amen."

Be Free to Succeed

When we love God, every day is like beginning life anew, because each day that we live in His love, we experience something fresh and wonderful that increases our zest for living. Each day the Lord reveals something more of Himself and the beauties of the world around us. Unfortunately many of us do not find this newness of life, because we pattern our lives on the norms of the society in which we live. As we look around us, we see people trying to find happiness in all kinds of human activities. Sometimes we learn by experience that happiness is not to be found in these things, but experience is an expensive and often a cruel teacher. However, joy is God's gift for His own people.

In order to hide out feelings of insecurity and inadequacy, we all wear masks of one kind or another to conceal what we truly are. We feel that we cannot let everyone know us as we really are. Perhaps to some intimate few, we lift our masks that they might glimpse our real personalities. Others we exclude and although they have known us for years, they have no actual idea of what goes on behind our masks. Even little children wear masks, appearing as sweet angels at home and mischievous imps when mother is not looking.

We all feel insecure in one way or another. Everyone is worried about the future and is afraid of being rejected and rebuffed. The fear of dread diseases troubles us. We know that for some life ends very abruptly at an early age. We have no guarantees that we will not be one of them.

In our culture, men are not supposed to cry. This is a tradition handed down from the ancient Germanic people. In some areas of the world, men weep openly. However, we are taught to hide our feelings, thoughts, and emotions. Some people find crying therapeutic. Others feel that one can express oneself in words so that there is no need to cry, if one can verbalize what is wrong so as to experience catharsis.

Our thoughts, emotions, and lives are important. What we do with our lives really matters. We should set our real selves free and cast aside all masks. Perhaps we are wearing a mask that shows us to be a person who is very macho. We act tough and do not reveal the loving, caring person that hides behind the mask. We hide our feelings so that people cannot hurt us and in order to "be a man." But wait. Let's take a look at our feelings. We are more than just macho. Perhaps we are sad, or troubled, worried, or afraid. We need to acknowledge our emotions and our fears and deal with them, if we want to be mentally and spiritually healthy. We need to remove our masks.

We need to look into our hearts and minds to see what we really are—people of value with feelings. In order to find happiness we have to arrive at being what God wants us to be. We are each a work of God—his unique gift to the world. We are beautiful in his sight. To some of us he has given physical beauty, however, we must understand that it is only part of us and that spiritual beauty is much more important.

Greatly influenced by peer pressure, we imitate friends and participate in the "culture of death," as John Paul II calls our depersonalized society, simply because others are. Troubled by many problems at home and on the job or at school, we cry out: "Life is difficult! It is not worth all the trouble it demands." Instead of feeling defeated at these times, let us turn to Christ and place all our difficulties in His hands. Problems are easy to solve when Christ dwells in us. Life in Christ is the most beautiful gift the Heavenly Father gives us. We hear people complain: "Christian life is difficult. There are no solutions for our problems. We have no future. The country is going to the dogs. There is no way out." Lies, all lies.

We have a wonderful future ahead of us constructing a life that can be truly marvelous. We need to begin to build a life that *is* worth the trouble. Bad news comes at us from every direction. The world is full of nay-sayers. We need to believe that the good far outweighs the evil in our world, for it really does.

One of the greatest evils in society today is violence. Tales of road rage are common as people take out their frustrations violently on those who annoy them in traffic. Violence is rampant today in the world. The Lord said a long time ago "all that take the sword shall perish with the sword" (Mt 26: 52). We do not use swords in our society today, but what Jesus says about swords also applies to guns and other weapons. People with guns in their hands use them against those who are closest and dearest to them. How often we have heard of fathers of families shooting all their children and then their wives and finally themselves. Unfortunately, eighty per cent of people who die from guns and other weapons are victims of domestic violence. Once we met a sweet old lady who many years ago killed her whole family with her husband's shotgun in a moment of madness.

When some hear of violence in the city streets and on the highways, they rush out and purchase a handgun and arm themselves with it every time they leave the house. Their attitude is this: "If anyone bothers me, I'll take care of them and give them something they aren't expecting." To be sure, the person who sets out to defend himself/herself with a gun does not have a very bright future.

The Holy Scripture shows us how to defend ourselves without resorting to weapons and violence. After wandering in the desert for forty years, the children of Israel are getting near to the Promised Land the Lord has planned for them. After directing Moses to go up on Mount Nebo from where he can see the Promised Land of Canaan in the distance, the Lord tells him that he, Moses, will not be permitted to enter the land because of a sin he committed and because he did not sanctify the Lord among the children of Israel (De 32: 49–52).

After the death of Moses, the Lord speaks to his successor, Joshua, telling him to cross the Jordan River with all his people into the land that He will give them, promising to deliver to them every place where they walk. The Lord instructs him as follows: "No man shall be able to resist you all the days of your life; as I have been with Moses, so will I be with you. I will not leave you, nor forsake you. Behold I command you, take courage, and be strong. Fear not and be not dismayed, because the Lord your God is with you in all things..." (Josh 1: 5–7). After telling Joshua that he is to divide the land by lots among the people of Israel, the Lord again commands him personally to be brave and fearless: "Take courage therefore, and be very valiant that you may observe and do all the law, which Moses my servant has commanded you. Turn not from it to the right hand or to the left, that you may understand all things, which you do. Let not the book of this law depart from your mouth, but you shall meditate on it day and night, that you may observe and do all things that are written in it" (Josh 1: 7). If Joshua does this, he can be assured of the Lord's guidance.

Before invading the land of Canaan, Joshua sends two spies to investigate the land and the fortified city of Jericho. They find lodging with a woman named Rahab, a prostitute, who turns out to be the heroine of the invasion.

When the King of Jericho learns from informants that two spies from the Israelites are at Rahab's house, he sends a messenger to her, saying: "Bring forth the men that came to you and have entered into your house, for they are spies, and are come to view all the land" (Josh 2: 3).

Having hidden the men by covering them with stalks of flax that she is drying, Rahab insists that the men have already left the city. She goes so far as to advise the king's messengers that if they hurry they can surely overtake them.

Before the two spies fall asleep for the night under the stalks of flax, Rahab goes to them and says she has heard of how the Red Sea parted so they could cross it when they left Egypt. She also heard of how they killed the two kings of the Ammorites, descendants of Lot. "I know that the Lord has given this land to you, for the dread of you is fallen upon us, and all the inhabitants of the land have lost all strength. We have heard that. And hearing these things we were frightened, and our hearts fainted away, neither did there remain any spirit in us at your coming in, for the Lord, your God, He is God in heaven above, and in the earth beneath" (Josh 2: 9–11).

In return for helping the two spies, Rahab asks for sanctuary for herself and her family and their possessions. After promising to grant them mercy, she lets them down to freedom with a scarlet cord she drops from her window near the wall of the city. The scarlet cord in her window will serve as a means for the children of Israel to recognize her and spare her.

Fortified with the information the spies brought him, Joshua and all the children of Israel move up close to the Jordan where they camp for three days. Then the people are directed to follow the Levitical priests who are bearing the Ark of the Covenant at a distance of about three thousand feet, being warned not to get too close, because the Lord had commanded people who were not priests not to touch the Ark for it would kill them to do so, as eventually happened to one Uzzah who tried to steady the Ark once when the oxen carrying it stumbled (1 Sam 7: 1). Moreover, sinful people were unable to look upon the Shekinah glory above the Ark and live (Lev: 16: 2).

The Ark of the Covenant was a chest measuring about 45 by 27 inches by 27 inches. Moses had it built according to God's specific directions. In addition to enclosing the two stones of the Ten Commandments, it held some of the manna that fed the people miraculously in the desert during their forty years of peregrination, and the rod of Moses' brother, Aaron, that budded with almond blossoms, indicating that the Lord gave authority to Aaron and Moses. During the wandering in the desert when they could find no water, the Lord told Moses to take this rod in hand and *command* water to flow from a certain rock. Instead of speaking to the rock, Moses struck it twice and water gushed out, but the Lord was displeased, because He had wished to demonstrate His power in a different way and for that reason neither Aaron nor Moses lived to enter the Promised Land (Num 20: 10).

The Ark of the Covenant, made of acacia wood, was covered both inside and out with gold. The lid of the Ark was a piece of gold, called the "place of mercy" (Ex 25: 17). Two cherubim were placed facing each other on the lid or "mercy seat" and God's presence, the Shekinah glory, was said to dwell between the cherubim. Once a year the high priest sprinkled the mercy seat with the blood of bulls and goats to make atonement for the sins of the people.

Carrying the Ark of the Covenant, the visible symbol of God's presence, on two poles that are fitted through rings on the sides of the Ark, the priests of Levi lead the way with Joshua encouraging the people with these words: "Be sanctified, for tomorrow the Lord will do wonders among you" (Josh 3: 5). When the priests enter the River Jordan, the waters stop flowing and although the river is flooding at that time of year, the people are able to cross easily over to the other side.

Finally, the Lord directs Joshua how they are to take the fortified city of Jericho. All the fighting men are to walk around the city once a day for six days. On the seventh day the priests are to take the seven jubilee trumpets while the children of Israel encircle the city seven times. The priests are to sound the trumpets while the people shout and the walls of Jericho will fall to the ground giving them free access to the city.

Something very interesting happens to Joshua; he experiences a theophany in which God appears to him as a man holding a drawn sword, introducing Himself to Joshua as the Prince of the Host of the Lord. Perceiving the Divine Presence, Joshua falls with his face to the ground and worships Him. Joshua then asks: "What says my Lord to His servant? Loose, says He, your shoes from off your feet, for the place where you stand is holy." Joshua did as he was commanded (Josh 5: 16).

Joshua and the children of Israel do as they were told, surrounding the city of Jericho, blowing the jubilee trumpets as directed and shouting. The walls tumble as the Lord had promised.

How do we relate this to our lives today? We all have our River Jordans to cross and Jerichos to conquer. Just as the Lord directed Joshua to believe valiantly and courageously in His promises and cross the Jordan, He is directing us today to have faith in His promises to be with us always and be strong and fearless and cross over the difficulties in our lives. We will enter not just a promised land, but also an eternal kingdom where peace, happiness and joy await. How do we cross our Jordans? Similar to the way in which Joshua and his people crossed. The Ark of the Covenant in the middle of the river signified God's covenant with His people. The Ark signified that Israel belonged to God and God to them. Because the people believed God would defend them, He did, without the use of weapons, as He directed.

We have far more than the Ark of the Covenant in our midst. The tabernacles in our churches that resemble the Ark of the Covenant, but containing exceedingly more than the manna of the Ark—they contain the Body and Blood of Christ. The power of the Blood of Christ shed on Calvary resides in every true believer in Christ. When faced with seemingly impossible obstacles, we need to plead the Blood of Jesus. If the Ark stopped the waters of the Jordan from flowing, how much more effective the Blood of Jesus will be in breaking the chains that prevent us from living happy productive lives! Let us invoke the power of the Blood when we think there is no resolution to our problems.

We want to make something of our lives so that they will count for good. We need to ask the Lord for strength and valor so that we can be fearless like Joshua and cross over all difficulties, remembering how He promised Joshua never to leave or abandon him. The same promise Jesus makes to each one of us (Heb 13: 5). He even appeared to Joshua and He promises us: "I will not leave you orphans, I will come to you" (Jn 14: 18).

The world tries to convince us of many negative things so that some of us come to believe the lies propagated. We believe we are ugly, too fat, worthless, unworthy, and stupid, among other things. This is simply not true. We are all works of God and are His children. As such we merit loving and to be loved in return. As His children, we merit to be free to become what He wishes us to be. No matter what people say about us, Jesus will defend us. Even if we have no money, no opportunity to get an education, or if we have some dread disease, the power of the Blood of Jesus far outweighs these things. The joy of the Lord does not depend on the color of our skin or any other external factor. It is grace freely given that flows directly into our hearts from the heart of God. His love and joy transform our lives; this is the great reality of life in Christ.

To cross the Jordan, we must have faith. Look what happened to the prostitute Rahab who had great faith and helped the children of Israel to make their crossing. She married Salmon, a prince of the tribe of Judah, and became the mother of Boaz and an ancestor of Jesus. She is cited for her faith in the great chapter on faith in the book of Hebrews (11: 31).

Let's cross the Jordan to the other side, leaving our problems behind. What city are we now going to conquer? Jericho. Joshua wanted to take up arms, but God told them they would triumph in a way that surprised everyone. Why did the Lord tell them to use trumpets instead of weapons? To test their faith. Similarly when we feel defeated, we cannot take up arms, rather we must rely of God's promises and the power of the Blood of Jesus. This is how we overcome the world—not with swords, nor by the strength of our own intelligence, but with the Spirit of God. "Not by might, nor by power, but by my spirit, says the Lord of Hosts" (Zec 4: 6).

Refusing to pay attention to the bad news of the world and its pessimism, we will trust in the Lord and we will receive the maximum God has to give us. The

Lord will stop our enemies in the midst of their machinations to destroy us, if we trust Him. As He took the children of Israel over the Jordan and delivered into their hands the fortified city of Jericho, He will do the same for us, if we persevere in the decisions we have made to construct our lives on the rock of Christ. From where does valor proceed? From the Word of God. If God be for us who can be against us? We are free to succeed—to become the people God wants us to be.

"Lord, we trust in your promises, knowing that with your help all things are possible. We will construct new lives, knowing that the power of the Blood of Jesus makes us invincible. We can do all things through Christ who gives us the strength. We want to receive the maximum of what You wish to give us. Make us people of courage and valor, setting us free to succeed in becoming the people You want us to be. Amen."

Be Free From Fear

Once during a time of national crisis, President Franklin D. Roosevelt told the American people: "The only thing we have to fear is fear itself." Freedom from fear is one of the most pressing human needs. Fear can paralyze us so that we defeat ourselves before we even try to surmount our difficulties. If we are going to be the effective people God created us to be, we need to be free from fear.

At the beginning of salvation history the Lord appears in a vision to Abram, later to be known as Abraham, greeting him with theses words: "Fear not, Abram, I am thy protector, and thy reward..." (Gen 15: 1). After this encounter almost every encounter between heaven and earth begins with the words "Fear not." When the Lord visits Abram, it is to bless him. When Abram complains of not having an heir, the Lord says to him: "Look up to heaven and number the stars, if you can... So shall your seed be" (Gen 15: 5). Next something wonderful happens when Abram believes God and what He tells him. The Scripture explains: "Abram believed God, and it was reputed to him unto justice" (Gen 15: 6). Because of his faith, God considers Abram to be a righteous man. Because of his belief in the promises of God, Abram fearlessly becomes our father in faith and the father of many nations.

In the time of Moses, the Lord begins instructing the people in holy fear. Repeatedly the phrase "Fear the Lord, your God" occurs in the book of Leviticus. This kind of fear is a gift of God and not the same kind of fear that we are trying to overcome. Neither is it a servile fear, but the fear the people of God should have of offending God who is so gracious and merciful to them. We read: "You shall not speak evil of the deaf, nor put a stumbling block before the blind, but you shall fear the Lord thy God, because I am the Lord" (Le 19: 14). A little later we read: "Rise up before the hoary head, and honor the person of the aged man and fear the Lord thy God. I am the Lord" (Le 19: 32). After a number of such directives of how the people are to follow the precepts of the Lord, the Lord promises them: "Do my precepts, and keep my judgments, and fulfill them, that you may dwell in the land *without any fear*" (Le 25: 18). Here the Lord clearly directs that if we want to live without any fear we must keep his commandments. He continues by saying that if the people walk in his precepts, He promises: "I will give peace in your coasts; you shall sleep, and there shall be none to make you afraid. I will take away evil beasts and the sword shall not pass through your quarters. You shall pursue your enemies, and they shall fall before you" (Le 26: 6–7). The Lord *will* defend his people. "Fear them not for the Lord your God will fight for you." (De 3: 22). Repeatedly the Holy Scripture assures us that the Lord will protect His people so that they need not fear. "Thou shall not fear them [enemies] because the Lord your God is in the midst of you, a God mighty and terrible" (De 7: 21).

By contrast, here is what the Lord will do to those who displease Him: "I will send fear in their hearts in the countries of their enemies, the sound of a flying leaf shall terrify them, and they shall flee as it were from the sword; they shall fall, when no man pursues them" (Le 26: 36). They shall be overcome with fear.

Throughout the Scripture the Lord continues to reassure His people that they are not to fear, that He is with them and will protect and defend them. As the Lord reassured Abraham and Moses, he also reassured Joshua. "Behold I command you, take courage and be strong. Fear not and be not dismayed, because the Lord your God is with you in all things whatsoever" (Josh 1: 9).

When Gideon encounters God, his experience is similar. "And the Lord said to him: Peace be with you; fear not, you shall not die" (Judg 6: 22). Gideon is afraid that he will die because he has seen the Lord face to face. When the angel of the Lord appears to Elijah, he counsels him not to be afraid (2 Kings 1: 15). King David, firmly believing in God, gives his son Solomon similar advice: "And David said to Solomon his son: 'Act like a man, and take courage, and do; fear not, and be not dismayed, for the Lord my God will be with you, and will not leave you, nor forsake you...'" (1 Chr 28: 20).

When someone tells King Jehoshaphat that a large invading army is coming from Edom to attack him, the King is very much alarmed and being seized with fear he determines to seek the Lord by proclaiming a fast for all of Judah. In a great assembly of people in the temple at Jerusalem, King Jehoshaphat prays this prayer: "O our God, wilt thou not then judge them? As for us, we have not strength enough to be able to resist this multitude, which comes violently upon us. But as we know not what to do, we can only turn our eyes to you" (2 Ch 20: 12).

As the multitude of men, women and children wait upon God to determine what course of action to take, the Spirit of the Lord comes upon the Levite Jahaziel, the son of Zechariah. "Thus says the Lord to you: Fear not, and be not dismayed at this multitude, for the battle is not yours, but God's (2ch 20: 15). We should always remember when fighting for a just cause that the battle is the Lord's and follow the example of King Jehoshaphat and the people of Jerusalem.

Before the battle, King Jehoshaphat and all the people of Jerusalem fall on the ground before the Lord in adoration (2 Ch 20: 18). Interestingly, the king appoints men to walk at the head of his army singing to the Lord and praising Him for the splendor of his holiness. As they sing: "Give glory to the Lord, for his mercy endures forever," the enemy is routed and defeated (2 Ch 20: 21).

We learn that when we are facing difficult obstacles, we overcome fear by trusting in God and His promises, praising Him for His everlasting mercy and the beauty of His holiness, realizing that the battle is His, not ours, and He will conquer our adversaries. When we become fearless, we become very powerful. The Holy Scripture tells us: "There is no power upon earth that can be compared with him who was made to fear no one" (Job 41: 24).

As we mentioned previously, King David was a man of great faith and a man who learned how to overcome fear. This can be very clearly seen in his psalms. Confidently he says: "The Lord is my light and my salvation, whom shall I fear? The Lord is the protector of my life: of whom shall I be afraid?" (Ps 25:1). When God is on our side, we do not need to fear anyone or anything. However David reminds us that we must have holy fear—fear of offending the Most High God. "O how great is the multitude of your sweetness, O Lord, which you have hidden for them that fear you!" (Ps 30: 20). David insists that the Lord will deliver those that fear Him. "The angel of the Lord shall encamp round about them that fear Him and shall deliver them" (Ps 33: 8). In this same psalm, the psalmist tells us: "Fear the Lord, all you his saints, for there is no want to them that fear Him" (33: 10). He assures us that if we fear the Lord and keep his precepts we will lack nothing and therefore we will have nothing to fear. We will not fear though the earth quakes and the mountains tumble into the sea. The psalmist advises us: "Cast your care upon the Lord and He shall sustain you" (54: 2).

David's son Solomon collected and polished many proverbs that express the wisdom of God in concise sentences, resembling parables; in fact, the Hebrew uses the same word for both proverb and parable. Practical guides on how one is to live daily life, proverbs are like the moral that is to be drawn from a parable. Especially to be held in high esteem because both Jewish and Christian traditions regard them as the inspired Word of God, the book of Proverbs has much to say about overcoming fear and trusting in God for His deliverance and protection. Here are a few examples:

But he shall hear me, shall rest without terror and shall enjoy my abundance without fear of evils. (Pr 1: 33)

If you sleep, you shall not fear; you shall rest, and your sleep shall be sweet. (Pr 3: 24)

Be not afraid of sudden fear, not of the power of the wicked falling upon you. (Pr 3: 25)

According to Proverbs one has no reason to fear anyone or anything if one fears the Lord and trusts in Him. "The fear of the Lord is unto life, and he shall abide in fullness without being visited with evil" (19: 23). If we fear the Lord, He will give us longer lives and the lives of the wicked will be shortened (10: 27). The fear of the Lord is described as "a fountain of life" that saves us from death (13: 27). "He that fears man shall quickly fall; he that trusts in the Lord shall be set on high" (29: 25).

Throughout salvation history, the themes of trusting in God for our deliverance and of not being afraid of anyone or anything continue to be constantly and continuously emphasized. The book of Isaiah has much to offer us in conquering fear. In fact, this prophet when speaking for God has very reassuring and comforting things to say to those who are suffering from fear, by revealing to us more of the compassionate love that is in the heart of God for his people and also the love of the people for God.

Beautifully, this prophet expresses his love for God in examples like the following: "Behold, God is my savior, I will deal confidently, and will not fear, because the Lord is my strength, and my praise, and He is become my salvation" (Is12: 2). Even more boldly, he proclaims the help of God for those in distress: "Say to the fainthearted, take courage, and fear not. Behold your God will bring the revenge of recompense. God Himself will come and will save you" (Is 35: 4). With a message in which he speaks directly for God he writes: "Fear not, for I am with you; turn not aside, for I am your God. I have strengthened you and have helped you and the right hand of my just one has upheld you" (Is 41: 10). Very tenderly, the prophet Isaiah tells us that God takes us by the hand and tells us not to fear (Is 41: 13).

According to Isaiah, God helps us and tells us not to fear, because he created us and redeemed and we belong to him. "Fear not for I have redeemed you and called you by your name; you are mine" (Is 43: 1). "Hearken to me, you that know what is just, my people who have my law in your heart; fear not the reproach of men, and be not afraid of their blasphemies" (Is 51: 7). When we have God's law in our hearts, we need not fear.

The prophet Jeremiah also promises God's deliverance to those who trust in Him. "Be not afraid at their presence, for I will make you not to fear their countenance (Jer 1: 7). "And I will deliver you in that day, says the Lord, and you shall not be given into the hands of the men whom you fear (Jer 39: 17). The prophet is equally convinced of the protection that God gives those that love Him, commanding them not to fear.

> And you, O son of man, fear not, neither be afraid of their words, for you are among unbelievers and destroyers, and you dwell with scorpions. Fear not their words, neither be dismayed at their looks, for they are a provoking house. (Ez 2: 6)

> I have made your face like adamant and like flint. Fear them not, neither be dismayed at their presence for they are a provoking house. (Ez 3: 9)

> Fear not, O man of desires, peace be to you. Take courage and be strong. And when he spoke to me, I grew strong and I said: Speak, O my Lord, for you have strengthened me. (Ez 10: 19)

In the New Testament, much more is revealed to us about overcoming fear, while maintaining the holy fear of the Lord in our hearts. When the angel appears to Joseph telling him that Mary has conceived a child of the Holy Spirit, his greeting is "Fear not" (Mt 1: 20). The same greeting is given to Zachary when the angel announces to him that his wife Elizabeth will bear him a son (Lk 1: 13). Mary hears the same greeting when the angel comes to her to announce that she is to be the mother of the Messiah (Lk 1: 30). The angels that sing with joy the night Christ is born announce the good news to the shepherds saying, "Fear not" (Luke 2: 10). Obviously God wants us to be unafraid.

When Jesus recruits his disciples like James and John, the sons of Zebedee, fishermen with Simon Peter, he says: "Fear not; from henceforth you shall catch men (Lk 5: 10). Throughout his entire ministry on earth, Jesus continually tells people not to fear. We are told not to fear those who can kill our bodies, but cannot kill our souls (Mt 10: 28). To Jesus our fear is a sign that we have little faith (Mt 8: 26). He reassures us as He did the people of the Bible: "Be of good heart; it is I, fear not" (Mt 14: 27). "Fear not, only believe" (Mk 5: 36). With much affection Jesus tells us, "Fear not, little flock, for it has pleased your Father to give you a kingdom" (Lk 12: 32).

So exactly how do we get fear out of our lives and hearts? We turn for the answer to the first epistle of John who instructs us that if our love is perfect we will have no fear. "Fear is not in charity, but perfect charity casts out fear, because fear has pain. And he that fears is not perfected in charity" (1 Jn 4: 18). If we want to be free from fear and the pain fear causes, we must love perfectly. How do we this? John tells us: "He that keeps His word, in him in very deed the charity of God is perfected; and by this we know that we are in Him" (1 Jn 2: 5). If we love Him, we will keep His word and He will perfect us in love.

John urges us to love one another, because love is from God and everyone who loves is born of God and knows Him (1 Jn 4: 7). "He that loves not, knows not God, for God is charity" (1 Jn 4: 8). If we want to know if we are truly born of God and know Him, all we have to do is ask ourselves if we love our brothers and sisters in Christ, for as St. John says: "He that says he is in the light, and hates his brother, is in darkness even until now" (1 Jn 2: 9). John goes on to explain in more detail how to know if love is perfect in us. "If we love one another, God abides in us, and his charity is perfected in us" (1 Jn 4: 12). Furthermore, we know that we abide in Him and He in us, because He has given us His Spirit (1 Jn 4: 13).

The Spirit that we have received liberates us from all fear. As St. Paul explains: "For you have not received the spirit of bondage again in fear, but you have received the spirit of adoption of sons, whereby we cry: Abba (Father)" (Rom 8:15). In his first letter to Timothy, Paul expands on this idea: "For God has not given us the spirit of fear, but of power, and of love, and of sobriety." If we are filled with the love of God and His Holy Spirit dwells in us, there is no room for fear in our hearts and minds. Therefore if we are tempted to fear, let us turn to the Word of God to overcome the temptation, because God does not want his people to be afraid.

What are the things that most often tempt us to fear? People all basically fear being rejected, rebuffed, and abandoned. We all need to be loved and tend to fear the loss of love that comes with rejection and abandonment. To fight this fear, we need to remember that Jesus has promised never to leave us or forsake us.

In recent years, the number of really virulent diseases has increased. We read of flesh destroying bacteria, of diseases like AIDS and West Nile Fever, of SARS, and antibiotic resistant strains of streptococcus and pneumonia, and, of course, the many kinds of cancer. To those of us who have fear about contracting disease, the Lord says: "If you will hear the voice of the Lord your God, and do what is right before Him, and obey his commandments, and keep all his precepts, none of the evils that I laid upon Egypt, will I bring upon thee: for I am the Lord thy healer" (Ex 15: 26). We must realize, however, that all healing in this world is temporary. Eventually, we all must die and when we do we will behold the Lord of Glory and He will heal all our infirmities. We will young again, strong, and in perfect health.

Fear of death has terrorized people down through the centuries. We who are in Christ have been delivered from the bondage of the fear of death. Because He is risen from the dead, we who are in Him will likewise rise from the grave to live forevermore with Him. Ours is a faith based on the historical witnesses of the first communities of Christians. In addition to the evidence of the resurrection of Christ found in the Bible, there is the witness of the Jewish historian Flavius Josephus (37–100 AD). He was the son of an aristocratic and priestly family related to the Hasmoneans, rulers of the Jewish people. He took the name Flavius from the family name of Emperor Vespasian, whose son Titus he accompanied to Jerusalem in 70 AD when the Romans destroyed the city. Although he implored the Jews to surrender, they held out against the Romans and were destroyed and the treasures of the temple were carted off to Rome by the conquerors.

After Josephus returned to Rome, Vespasian granted him Roman citizenship and a pension, making it possible for him to write the history of the Jews. In his book *The Jewish War* he described the conflict between the Romans and the Jews from the time of Antiochus Epiphanes to just after the fall of Jerusalem. Around the year 94, he wrote what many consider to be his most significant work, *Antiquities of the Jews* in twenty volumes. What is of most interest to us is that he wrote about John the Baptist, describing his baptism of people whom he exhorted to turn to God. He records that Herod had him incarcerated in the castle Macherus and put to death (Josephus *Antiquities* 15: 5 2). He also records the arrest of the Apostle James and some of his companions that were ordered to be stoned (Josephus 20: 9 1). Most significant to us is that he recorded the crucifixion and resurrection of Jesus.

> Now there was about this time Jesus, a wise man, if it be lawful to call him a man; for he was a doer of wonderful works, a teacher of such men as receive the truth with pleasure. He drew over to him both many of the Jews and many of the Gentiles. He was [the] Christ. And when Pilate, at the suggestion of the principal men amongst us, had condemned him to the cross, those that loved him at the first did not forsake him, for he appeared to them alive again the third day, as the divine prophets had foretold these and ten thousand other wonderful things concerning him. And the tribe of Christians, so named from him, are not extinct at this day. (Josephus 18: 3 1)

In addition to the historical witness of Josephus, St. Paul recounts that after the resurrection, Jesus appeared to Simon Peter and then to the twelve apostles and finally to five hundred people who saw Him at one time, and then to James and all of the apostles and finally to Paul himself. Paul mentions that at the time that he was writing about it, many of the witnesses to the resurrection were still alive (1 Cor 15). If what Paul had written concerning the appearances of Jesus after the resurrection were not true, many people could have come forth and contradicted him. We accept him as a reliable witness and with him we exclaim, "O death, where is thy victory? O death, where is thy sting? Death is swallowed up in victory" (1 Cor 15: 54–5).

St. Paul tells us that to die is gain and that we gain much when we dissolve to be with Christ. Fearlessly, he met death by the sword during Nero's persecution of the Church in Rome, knowing that He was entering into the joy of the Lord. We should not fear death, for Christ has conquered death.

The world and human institutions are filled with a spirit of fear. If we avoid them as much as possible, we will be less tempted to fear. Jesus and the people of God offer us solidarity against fear. The things we are most apt to fear often never happen. Our minds are filled with phantasms that try to rob us of our peace of soul. Let Jesus banish them by reading His Word and listening to Him say to us, "Fear not, I am here." We do not need to fear wars and terrorism as long as we hold fast to Jesus. Let us hold fast to His promises to deliver us from all our fears and lead us into His eternal kingdom of love, peace and joy. Let us seek His truth and let Him set us free from all fear.

Love Sets Us Free

Love is the most important and effective cure that exists. We all need it, but we must be on guard that our love does not become an obsession, for then it is no longer love, but a passion. Our culture floods our world with love songs, but their ideas of love are far different from those of the Word of God that come largely from the writings of St. Paul and other New Testament writers. Love is the better, the more excellent way, says St. Paul (1 Cor: 13). We can do something very wonderful, but the Holy Scripture tells us that if we do not do it with love, it is worth nothing. Even if we give everything we have to feed the poor, it is a worthless act, if we do not do it for love.

Many think that love is a sentiment—a feeling. Not so! A sentiment is a passing thing, a fleeting feeling that is evanescent like low lying clouds on a foggy morning that are chased away when the sun comes up. Love is something far more than that. To be true love, it must be a well-considered and resolute decision to make someone happy. We decide to do good or procure good for the person we love. It is the decision to sacrifice ourselves for those we love.

Love understands. It is never envious, nor presumptuous, nor egoistic. When we love someone, we excuse their faults and always think the best of them. Love serves the welfare of the chosen other and seeks always to please him/her.

We can examine ourselves by reading St. Paul's description of love to see how we rate (1 Cor 13). One of the most important criteria for someone who loves is the desire to serve. There is nothing sadder in a relationship than when one party refuses to serve. Parents should teach their children to serve. Unfortunately, in some homes there is very little understanding and the children are taught to receive a great deal, but not to give. Are we rearing a generation of little egoists by giving them every thing they want? We need to teach them to serve as well as to receive.

We need to pray to receive the charism of love—true love such as St. Paul describes it. When we love in this way we can love all people and rejoice over the good things of our friends and, yes, even rejoice over the good things of our enemies. Love is not envious. We want to be neither envious nor envied. Such love gives us interior peace. Actually it is foolish to envy people, because we do not know what is really going on in their lives. Faces do not tell us what hearts and souls are feeling.

True love frees us to be happy every minute of every day of our lives. Such love opens our hearts to receive joy from God as His love bubbles up within us and overflows to those around us.

We should treat everyone kindly as if it were the last day of their lives or ours. We should love them as if we were all going to die tomorrow. Unfortunately, if we spoke to our friends the way we do, at times, to members of our families, we would have no friends. When we have true love in our hearts, we will treat all with courtesy and tenderness. If we do this, there will be far fewer scars in peoples' hearts needing to be healed, for love cures and takes away the pains that we all experience in life almost on a daily basis. If you don't believe love heals, watch a little child run to its mother for her to kiss away the little pain it gets when it falls down. In a hospital, watch as someone lays a hand on the brow of a patient and immediately his pain become more bearable. Love cures—love takes away pain.

In loving someone, we must remember we can never possess him/her. People are free. They belong only to God. The more we try to manipulate those we love, the more apt we are to lose them and the unhappier we will be. When we truly love someone, we suffer all we have to for that person—enduring everything that we must. We love them no matter what they do or what might happen to them. So many times we have seen men leave their wives because the women contracted serious chronic disease, often deserting them to fend for themselves and their children at a time when they were least able to do so. These men did not know how to love and sacrifice themselves for love. All is done easily with love and when we love time passes very fast.

The love of all loves is when two people love each other in God. They love each other in Him and love Him in each other. Great happiness is found in such love. They have found the charism of love and the joy they experience is a taste of heaven. They are truly blessed.

The charism of love gives us a new attitude. By nature we are proud, envious, and self-seeking, but the charism of love changes us so that we become free to love with the beautiful love that God inspires and infuses into our souls.

The greatest thing in life is to believe in God. His greatest gift to us is the ability to love with unconditional love. We say to the one we love "I love you as you are." That is the way God loves us. We tell the one we love, "I do things for you because I love you." Jealousy never enters into this kind of love, for it is torment.

We tell the one we love, "I am with you today freely and will be every day forever, not because of your need or mine, but because I love you."

When the one we love is in pain, we remember that love is therapeutic.

The soul that is wounded and hurting needs to be bathed in love with a healing love such as St. Paul describes (1 Cor 13). This perfect true love will last forever. St Paul ensures us that love endures into the life of the world to come. The Holy Scripture tells us "Love is strong as death" (Song 6: 8)

"Lord we want to experience this beautiful love. Please give us the charism of love that we may love in this way with a love that begins now and endures forever, for we know such love never dies. Make us free to love in a love that is freely given and freely received. Amen."

Be Free From Suffering!

Most of us are the cause of our own needless suffering. We suffer because we are blind to the very spiritualities that will set us free. When we have true spiritual vision, suffering will leave us. We will still have pain; it is very real and is always part of life. All living creatures experience pain. However, we view suffering as an attitude. The way we regard pain totally changes the way we experience it. How we understand the difficulties and tribulations of life can make the difference between suffering and being free from suffering.

One of the main causes of our suffering is that we have certain expectations—ways of thinking about ourselves and the people and things around us. When our expectations are not met, we suffer, because we think things have to be in a certain way. Perhaps we want a house in a certain neighborhood, but it is beyond our financial means. We cannot have it and so we suffer. Perhaps we want a certain honor and it passes us by and so we suffer. We make rules for our families and ourselves and when they are not complied with, we suffer. The fault is ours. We can suffer because someone dropped cigar ashes on our carpet. Even tragedies can result because expectations are not met.

We can have wishes, interests, and desires, but in order to keep suffering from our lives, we have to renounce the power these have over us. To live free of the suffering of uncontrolled desires, all we have to do is submit to the will of God for our lives. It is the only way to find happiness. His plan for our lives is almost always different from ours. To find happiness, we must remove all negative thinking from our minds. Negative thinking is often expressed when people say: "I don't like..." or "Why does all this happen to me..." or "I never get anything I want." Negativity is a mode of thinking that causes us to suffer.

Everyone does not encounter reality in the same way that other people do. What differentiates one person's view of reality from another's is the way in which he looks at things. When we have absolute faith in God, the way we regard life and its events is in an absolutely peaceful way, because we know that everything is in the hands of the Lord.

In the Holy Scripture, three Jewish young men have much to teach us about avoiding suffering. During the Babylonian captivity, Shadrack, Meshach, and

Abednego defied the law of the land by refusing to bow down and worship a golden idol. Upon penalty of death requiring anyone who defies the law to be burned in a fiery furnace, the three young men realize they have nothing to lose. They will not bow to the pagan idol and commit sin. They respond to the Babylonian king, that their God can deliver them from all evil, but even if He does not, they will not bow down and worship the statue. After the Babylonians throw them in the furnace and make it hotter than usual, they see a fourth person in the furnace with the three young men. Awestruck, the Babylonians let the three out of the fiery furnace and find that they are completely unharmed and that smoke does not even cling to their garments.

How are we to understand this story? The three Jews knew they had nothing to lose and consequently they were fearless. We believe that we possess many things. We believe the family is ours, money is ours, and even our body is ours. We need to understand that in reality we possess nothing and that everything is in the hands of God. We submit to the will of God; when we are in trouble, it is His choice whether to rescue us or not. Our Christian faith tells us that Jesus, the Son of God, walks with us every moment of our lives. So what do we have to do to be set free from suffering? We have to lose our fear, like the three Jews in the furnace. They were absolutely unafraid.

Our faith is based on the greatness and the truth of Jesus Christ our Savior. To be happy and stop suffering we must come to the light of Christ and eliminate envy, negativity, evil speaking, hatred, and all other harmful things from our lives. Moreover, we must realize that life is a great gift of God and submit to His plan for how we are to live it. Nothing else will bring us happiness.

Nothing in life is exactly the way we would like it to be. Why make ourselves miserable about little things that are unimportant, especially if we have no power to change them? A few ashes dropped on the carpet by a guest in our home should not be the cause of suffering. The only attitude that will permit us to be happy is one in which we do everything for the love of God, always living in the Eternal Now of God's presence. This moment is the only one we possess.

We all encounter many fiery furnaces in life. If God is with us, He will get us out of the hot spots. And He has promised always to be with us and never to forsake us. All our daily worries are for naught. All our negative thinking robs us of the joy that God wants to give us. Let us stop suffering now—this very day. How? Simply yield to the will of God. Submit! We must not let things make us bitter. If we are ill, He may cure us or not. Either way we will yield to His will. If our spouse snores, we will buy earplugs, and not let it disturb our peace. We have absolute control over our thoughts, desires, and actions. We must decide to be happy and stop suffering. Nothing can make us unhappy, if we do not let it. No one can make us suffer, if we do not let him or her do so.

People can give us pain, but we can control pain by eliminating our desires and expectations. We control everything we think and feel. If we submit to Jesus Christ and His will, most of the things that cause us trouble are not important. We must realize that we can stop suffering this very day if we let Jesus Christ and His will for our lives take precedence over everything else. Let us begin by thanking Him for all we are and have—health, strength, families, friends, and necessities of life, especially thanking Him for feeding us with His Word and His saving Presence.

St. Paul tells us what we have to do to live a joyful life—we have to love. Without love, everything is worthless. Even if we have faith that will move mountains, it is worthless if we do not have love in our souls. The devils of hell believe in God; they have faith and even tremble at the thought of Him, but they do not and cannot love Him.

Love makes it possible for us to be set free from suffering. The Holy Scripture tells us: "Fear is not in charity, but perfect charity casts out fear, because fear has pain. And he that fears is not perfected in charity" (1 Jn 4: 18). Love drives out fear and all its pain. If we have learned to handle pain and difficulties, we are coming to the light.

How do we know if we are in the light? We ask ourselves whether the loves in our life are producing pain or joy. If the answer is pain, we have not yet come into the light of Christ. If we are suffering because of what is taking place in our emotional life, in our life as a Christian, or in our relationships, we need to ask the Lord for a new birth. We need to understand that in order to be His disciples we have to deny ourselves. Self denial is the root of freedom, for the less we want the more we can possess in peace.

One can become enamored with someone and have in one's imagination an idea of the person that is completely false; this is passion. In time the relationship will die when the lover sees the beloved as s/he really is. Often falling in love is an illusion that ends in infatuation and obsession.

If we are afraid the person that we think we love will discover something about us that will damper his/her ardor, what we have is not love; it is merely a relationship that will cause us suffering. Dissimulation always causes suffering, for there is nothing worse that deceiving someone. If we are hiding anything from our beloved, we will not be happy, because we are afraid of having our secret discovered. Perfect love has no fear.

When we love someone as s/he is, we become free to enjoy our love. Love is a gift of God; it is divine. The way of perfect love is the way of joy. Anything less than perfect love leads to envy, manipulation, frustration, and unhappiness. If someone loves us knowing all about us, our love is authentic. True love is not based on need. Phrases like "I need you," or "I can't live without you" are very selfish and deceptive. They simply are not true and for this reason such an attitude can lead to disaster. True love accepts the beloved just as s/he is.

Because perfect love casts out all fear and we want our love to be perfect, it is important to try to get rid of fear when we love someone. In order for fear to vanish from our relationship we need to give the person we love the assurance that we will never abandon or leave him/her, just as the Lord promises never to leave or abandon us. When we love someone and that person loves us, we must give him/her some assurance that our love for him/her is unconditional so that the person can be secure in our love, knowing that no matter what happens, we will stay with them. We want those that love us to be reassured that our love for them is undying. If the people we love feel insecure in our relationship, how can our love grow?

Unrequited love is most painful and we need to let people know how much we love them and that our love is eternal— "as strong as death." They should not have to simply assume that we love them. All too often people say: "Of course, I love you. Can't you see all the things I do? Doesn't that tell you that I love you?"

What destroys love is the attempt to control and govern the beloved. So that our love will never die, we have to renounce trying to possess and control those we love. We cannot possess anyone. The attempt to possess destroys the loveliness and enchantment of the relationship.

We must remember that if we are suffering we are not doing the will of God. Some people enjoy pain and suffering; they are masochists and are really ill. One's suffering indicates to what degree we are close to God's plan for our lives. Suffering is the product of our attitudes; we choose to suffer. Pain, in contradistinction, is something we don't hope for, such as cancer or a divorce.

Scripture shows us the marvelous power of God when he is directing us. We are thinking of how Jesus comes to the apostles who have been fishing all night and catching no fish. He tells them to put down their nets one more time and they probably do so to humor Him, believing that they will not catch anything and to their amazement the net is overflowing with fish. For God to direct our lives we need to receive and treasure His Word in our hearts. The Holy Scripture tells us: "The words of the Lord are pure words, as silver tried by the fire, purged from the earth refined seven times." (Ps 11: 7). The Word of God is powerful, living, and efficacious. Speaking for God the Prophet Isaiah writes about the Word of God: "So shall my Word be, which shall go forth from my mouth; it shall not return to me void, but it shall do whatsoever I please, and shall prosper in the things for which I sent it" (Is 55: 11). God's Word is truth (Jn 17: 17). The Scripture also tells us: "For the Word of God is living and effectual, and more piercing than any two edged sword; and reaching unto the division of the soul and the spirit, of the joints also and the marrow, and is a discerner of the thoughts and intents of the heart" (Heb 3: 12).

The Word of God shows us what is correct, authentic, important and true. When we confront our lives with the Word of God and the plan of God, we see the importance they have in leading us to happiness by showing us what God indicates and commands. We see that our attitudes have been formed throughout our lives by ideas, prejudices, desires that come from the world and are in opposition to God's Word and plan and are the cause of our unhappiness.

Our desires are not necessarily bad. They become harmful when they create dependencies—things and people we feel we need to be happy. We absolutely must rid ourselves of these dependencies. Many desires are good. A desire to eat, to earn a living, to protect one's family—these are all good desires. Actually desire is the key to progress in society. However, when a desire creates a dependency that is necessary for us to be happy, the desire is converted into perdition or tragedy, because it is then the key to unhappiness. Nothing or no one can guarantee our happiness and when we have to depend on anyone or anything to be happy we will be unhappy.

Happiness is within us because the Kingdom of Heaven is within (Lk 17: 21). God is within us. We know that God is love because the Holy Scripture tells us that He is. It also tells us that God created us in His image and likeness. This does not mean that God has two hands and two feet like we have, but rather that we, like Him, are love. God is love and WE ARE LOVE. We are created in the image of God and St. John says that God is love. The more we strive to increase love in our hearts, the more we will be like God. Love is infinitely perfectible; there is no limit to the degree of love we can possess within us.

Many of us are unhappy because we do not understand that we are love and that we have been created to love. Other people are so completely corrupted by the baseness of our society that it is impossible for them to demonstrate the love God created them to give and to receive. In order to be happy and free from suffering we must live the reality that we are love.

Dependencies that are created by unchecked desires will block love and happiness from springing forth in our souls. Because we spend our lives seeking to satisfy our dependencies—to have things just the way we desire them to be—we do not realize that we are love and we are happiness. Happiness is not contingent upon external factors. It is the kingdom of heaven within us.

How can we find this kingdom of happiness within and set ourselves free from suffering? We have to deprogram our minds. We have been programmed to be unhappy by the world in which we live. We tend to think that we will be happy when some event occurs in our lives, such as, for example, finding a new job, buying a bigger car, moving to a finer house, getting married, or having a baby. God wants us to be happy NOW. We have been created in the image and likeness of God and redeemed by the blood of Jesus to live in communion with the Eternal Father who is love. We must reprogram our minds to this new realization. We are love! All aspects of our lives prevent us from seeing the reality of what we are. Our culture is responsible for our not seeing the reality of God and His divine life and love within us. Culture has some good aspects and some very negative components. Great music and literature are a cultural blessing. However, such cultural factors as aggressive sexism, whether male or female, is an enemy of happiness. We must rid ourselves of all the false "isms" of our culture, if we are to realize that God made us for love and we are love.

Some people say that life is hard. There is nothing wrong with life; it is our thinking about it that make it seem difficult. We have to deprogram ourselves getting rid of all the false notions that we have absorbed from our society. We have to eliminate phantasms of nostalgia that try to rob us of our happiness by making us believe something in the past was better for us than what we have today. The memory might be good but the nostalgia is not. Let us accept the past as part of our lives, but reject it as a dependency. The past is over; we must let it go. Perhaps there remains within us a child who suffered many indignities and needs to be comforted before we can let go of the past completely. One way to do this is to picture ourselves as we are now—mature and wise—talking to that child, giving it understanding and offering compassion and gentle love.

In reprogramming ourselves, we recognize that we are a manifestation of God's love and that He created us for love, using our parents as instruments of His creation. We acknowledge that He has pardoned us and lifted us to spiritual tranquility. We realize that the most important thing we can do is to discover God's plan for our happiness. For this knowledge we go to His Word, the Holy Scripture. We begin to know His Word, receive it into our hearts, and conform our lives to it. As we begin to live His Word, we conform our lives to it, saying: "We submit to the beautiful plan you have for our lives." The moment when we accept God's will, happiness begins to break forth in us, for we know that everything we are and have is in the hands of God who loves us with an unfailing love. Receiving the Word of God and conforming our lives to it brings a manifestation of the best and most beautiful blessings that we have received from God our Father. The way to freedom from suffering and happiness is obedience to God's will for our lives.

Why are so many people unhappy? Because psychologically it is much easier to put the responsibility for being happy on other people, instead of taking responsible for our own happiness. Why should we wait for other people to make us happy? When we blame others for our unhappiness, we shift the blame from ourselves to them. How many times have we heard people say: "I am unhappy because someone did thus and so to me"? Our happiness is our own; we control it. And we control our programming. No one can take away our peace and happiness; no one can change what we are. Only we can do that. We don't need anyone or anything to be happy. The kingdom of heaven is within us. What we like and what we do not like are insignificant. We accept what we have, getting rid of all our negativity.

We each have a personality and we should pray to God that we may reveal our true personality—we are love, we are happiness. We don't have to compete with anyone. We do what needs to be done, embrace what is happening today, forgetting the past and placing the future in the hands of God.

Let us thank God that He made us to be love as He is love. Let us get rid of all the roots of unhappiness—expectations, negativity and dependencies. Let us forget the defects we see in others; they usually are defects we ourselves possess. Let us live in God's love and truth, fully realizing that we are love, we are happiness. We have all we need within us and it is love.

Holy Scripture tells us how we shall be blessed if we put our trust in God.

> Blessed be the man that trusts in the Lord, and the Lord shall be his confidence. And he shall be as a tree that is planted by the waters, that spreads out its roots towards moisture, and it shall not fear when the heat comes. And the leaf thereof shall be green, and in the time of drought it shall not be solicitous, neither shall it cease at any time to bring forth fruit." (Jer 17: 7–8)

In other words, if we trust in the Lord we shall lack nothing. What does the water symbolize? It is the Word of God, the grace of God, and the presence of God in our lives. We are nourished by the doctrine of Jesus, the Word and the presence of Jesus, infused with the gifts of the Holy Spirit so that we live the beatitudes.

Blessed are the poor in spirit, for theirs is the kingdom of heaven. Blessed are the meek, for they shall possess the land. Blessed are they that mourn, for they shall be comforted. Blessed are they that hunger and thirst after justice, for they shall have their fill. Blessed are the merciful, for they shall obtain mercy. Blessed are the clean of heart, for they shall see God. Blessed are the peacemakers, for they shall be called children of God. Blessed are they that suffer persecution for justice's sake, for theirs is the kingdom of heaven. Blessed are you when they shall revile you, and persecute you, and speak all that is evil against you, untruly, for my sake. Be glad and rejoice, for your reward is very great in heaven. (Mt 5: 3–12)

In conclusion, to set ourselves free from suffering and attain the happiness of the beatitudes, we need to realize that pain is very real, but suffering is a decision we make that is the product of wrong attitudes. We must get rid of our expectations, dependencies, and negativity. We must choose to be free of suffering. When we submit to the will of God we begin to find freedom.

We possess true liberty when we can control everything that comes into our minds so that we will harbor nothing within us that is contrary to the will of God. Above all we must renounce sin, for it is slavery. Free people do not have to sin. "Whosoever abides in Him, sins not; and whosoever sins, hath not seen Him, nor known Him" (1 Jn 3: 6). Free people escape the slavery of sin. Only people who are free find the kingdom of heaven within. Only they know how to stop suffering by adhering to God's will, eliminating all expectations, dependencies, and negativity from their lives.

Jesus came to reconcile us with all creation as we embrace His plan for our happiness. He delivers us from all appearances of reality, so that we can embrace His reality and live a live of joy and happiness, set free from suffering. Yes, there will still be pain, but it will be manageable.

It is important to remember that if we do not become attached to anything, we will not have anything we have to renounce. We should live knowing that eventually we will lose everything we have. The only thing we can take with us when we enter the life of the world to come is love.

Let us thank God for all that He has given us and enjoy it now. We should not be sad at losing it when we die, because we will be entering into a life that will be far more glorious where the Lord will provide everything we need to be happy. The more love we take with us into eternity, the greater will be our beatitude and more poignantly we will be able to embrace others in an irresistible love that will never die.

Now let us consider some specific and practical ways to go about deprogramming ourselves so that we can set ourselves free from suffering. We need to begin every day by placing our lives into the loving hands of God. Doing this will bring us tranquility. We embrace joyfully the lives God has given us, remembering that Christ suffered for us all and we do not have to suffer for anyone, but rather we will love everyone and try to help all.

We recommend setting aside an hour each day to nourish our spiritual and psychological growth. A half-hour spent in praying, reading the Word of God, and meditating is really necessary. If we live near a church, we might spend our half hour there praying before the reserved Eucharist. This is a wonderful practice that becomes even more blessed the more often we do it. Only someone who has spent a lot of time praying to Jesus in this special way knows the beatitude that comes with it. It is not necessary to say much. Just a few words will suffice. We begin by telling Jesus that we love Him. Then we wait to experience His presence in our souls. When we find Him present within us, there is no need for further conversation, for He picks us up on the wings of Love, the Holy Spirit, and infuses our souls with His wisdom and knowledge, imparting to us whatever He knows we need. Before we leave our time of prayer before the tabernacle, we turn our attention to the Heavenly Father, thanking Him for giving us Jesus, our way, truth and life. We also remember to commune with the Love that unites us, the Holy Spirit. We end our prayer with joyful praises of the Holy Immortal Trinity.

The other half hour can be spent doing something we enjoy doing. Perhaps one might play a musical instrument, take a walk, or chat with a good friend. We need this time to get in touch with ourselves. If we spend all our time on the run, we have no time to think. Whatever we do it should be pleasurable.

We should live our personal lives one day at a time, not concerned about the past or solicitous about the future, remembering that He is the Lord of time and all is in His hands. If our day is not going well, we will act as though it were. Every day we will do something good for someone without expecting any gratitude or return of any kind. To expect to be repaid would be a cause of unhappiness and perhaps suffering for us. We will not let anyone spoil our day by unkind words or deeds, immediately rejecting their negative attitudes and commending them to God. We will live free from suffering in the light of God's love and truth.

"Lord, we beseech you to give us the charism of love as we renounce our desires to possess, manipulate, and control those we love. We thank You for all we have and all we are—health, life, strength, friends, necessities of life, and above all for the gift of love. We especially thank you for feeding us with your Word, Your saving presence, and Your Body and Blood, Soul and Divinity in the

Eucharist. Lord Jesus, we accept You in our hearts. We accept Your Word and yield and submit to Your will, to whatever You desire. We renounce our expectations, our desires and their dependencies, and our negativity. We receive Your Word with the joy that is in Your presence. We are afraid of nothing. Your love has driven all fear from our minds and hearts. We are not afraid of loneliness, rejection, criticism, old age, illness, pain, lack of money, or even death, because You, Lord Jesus, are with us. We are not afraid of anything. We are happy in the name of Jesus. We have strength and fortitude. We thank You, Lord, that no one can take Your peace from our hearts. Nothing can make us angry or unhappy because we belong to You and all bitterness leaves our hearts.

"We praise, You, Lord, that you set us free. Fill us with Your joy, and take away all bitterness and unhappiness. We want to give You our best as gifts. This is the day You have made, Lord, we will rejoice and be glad in it. We bless you for this intimate moment. We thank You for giving us the gift of love. Thank you for teaching us that suffering in love comes from desiring to control those we love and when we do control and have expectations, dependencies, and negative thoughts we are not perfect in love. Perfect our love, Lord.

"Lord, we renounce all our desires, manipulation, jealousy, anxieties in our relationships and accept those we love just as they are. We are together because we love them, not because of any need. Let us be free and at peace from this day forward, as we accept this teaching as the key to happiness.

"Jesus, we thank you that you made us for love, and that our parents conceived us in love. We thank You that you created us in Your image and likeness. We renounce the programming of our culture—egoism, feminism, chauvinism, and all the other "isms" that keep us from realizing that You created us to love. We are Your children, created in Your image and likeness—we are love. We receive Your peace into our hearts. No problem, no person, nothing can take away the peace You give us. Only our own thoughts can destroy our peace. Permit us, Lord, to realize who we are in You and who You are in us. Amen."

Be Free from Anger

If anger is not cut out at its roots and is permitted to remain in the soul, it is like a venomous snake curled and ready to unleash its venom at the least provocation. For good reason, the Apostle Paul tells us: "Let all bitterness, and anger, and indignation, and clamor, and blasphemy be put away from you, with all malice. And be kind one to another, merciful, forgiving one another, even as God has forgiven you in Christ (Eph 4: 31–32).

From the earliest days of the Church, people have struggled with anger and have analyzed it, dissected it, and found ways to subdue it. Hermas, the brother of Pope St. Pius I (140–154) wrote decisively about anger and its destructive powers that destroy the servants of God:

> Now, in the first place, violent anger is foolish, frivolous and silly. In the next place, bitterness arises from silliness, from silliness wrath, from wrath, anger, and from anger rage. Finally, the rage that has in it such evil elements becomes a serious and incurable sin. For, when all such spirits dwell in one vessel along with the Holy Spirit, it cannot hold them, but overflows. Then the delicate spirit that is not accustomed to dwell with an evil one, nor with uncouthness, departs from a man of this kind and tries to dwell in a gentle, calm abode. (268)

Obviously anger, which begets rage, is a very serious sin since it causes the Holy Spirit to depart from us.

To turn their attack on us back on themselves, Tertullian (ca 155–220), the first of the Latin theological writers, has an interesting approach in the use of patience in dealing with adversaries who in their rage would inflict pain on us. Because we carry about our souls and bodies, exposed to injury from any who would attack us, he counsels patience, not anger in dealing with them, recalling that the Lord says we are to turn the other cheek when smitten on the face. He recommends that if some one assails us with curses or reproach, that we respond by quoting the Lord's own words: "Blessed are you when they shall revile you, and persecute you, and speak all that is evil against you, untruly, for my sake. Be glad and rejoice, for your reward is very great in heaven" (Mt 5: 11–12). He then adds an interesting comment about the "pleasure of patience."

> For every injury, whether inflicted by tongue or hand, when it has lighted upon patience, will be dismissed with the same fate as, some weapon launched against and blunted on a rock of most steadfast hardness. For it will wholly fall then and there with bootless and fruitless labor, and sometimes will recoil and spend its rage on him who sent it out, with retorted impetus. No doubt the reason why anyone hurts you is that you may be pained; because the hurter's enjoyment consists in the pain of the hurt. When then you have upset his enjoyment by not being pained, he must needs be pained by the loss of his enjoyment. Then you not only go unhurt away, which even alone is enough for you; but gratified, into the bargain, by your adversary's disappointment and revenged by his pain. This is the utility and the pleasure of patience. ("Of Patience" Ch 8)

Tertullian goes on to explain in chapter ten that if we rely on patience, we will feel no pain and if we feel no pain, we will not desire to avenge ourselves against the person who assaulted us. He points out that we are not allowed to remain one day without patience, because the apostle says we are not to let the sun go down on our anger (Ch 13). Where God is, according to Tertullian, we will always find His foster-child, Patience (Ch 15). This means that when the Holy Spirit is present, patience is always with Him.

Another early Christian writer who dealt with anger was John Cassian, who, although he was never canonized, was regarded as a saint by Pope St. Gregory the Great. He was born in what is today the southern part of France, Provence, about the year 360 and died about 435, most likely near Marseilles. While he was still a young man, he traveled, accompanied by an older friend, one Germanus, to Palestine, where they lived in cells in Bethlehem. Having wealthy parents who provided him with a good education and encouraged his inquiring mind, John Cassian and his friend then went to Egypt to learn the secrets of sanctity from the famous desert saints. In Egypt, they collected the material that John was later to publish under the titles of "Conferences" and "Institutes." Later traveling to Constantinople, he met St. John Chrysostom who raised him to the deaconate and put him in charge of caring for the treasures of the cathedral. He was elevated to the priesthood later in Rome and spent the end of his life near Marseilles where he founded two monasteries.

In his "Conferences," Cassian observes that anger results in all kinds of evil—murder, strife, heresy, theft, bearing false witness, blasphemy, surfeiting, drunkenness, back-biting, buffoonery, filthy conversation, lying, perjury, foolish talking, scurrility, restlessness, greediness, bitterness, clamor, wrath, contempt, murmuring, temptation, despair, and many other faults.

In the "Insitutes," he proceeds to give incisive directions on how to deal with anger. He states that as long as this "deadly poison" remains within, it blinds the soul, making it impossible for the soul to partake of wisdom, or even attain to eternal life. This, although severe, is in keeping with the teaching of the Church, which always considered anger to be one of the seven deadly sins that can destroy the soul that does not reject it.

Speaking of what St. Paul said about not letting the sun go down on our anger, John Cassian relates it to Amos 8: 9: "And it shall come to pass in that day, says the Lord God, that the sun shall go down at midday, and I will make the earth dark in the day of light." To John Cassian, this passage of Holy Scripture signifies that because our reason can be compared to the sun, those that are angry find that their sun sets at midday. "The mind, that is the reason, which is fairly called the sun because it looks over all the thoughts and discernings of the heart, should not be put out by the sin of anger." In teaching that anger should never enter into the heart of man, Cassian explains that this teaching has been handed down by the elders of the desert to show how they felt about it, because "they do not permit it even for a moment to effect an entrance" into the heart" (Ch X).

Observing that there are some who let their anger continue for days after the sun has set—they have lost their reason—he remarks that they have rancor in their hearts while professing to be no longer angry, but still refuse to speak pleasantly. By not openly showing their anger, they drive the poison of anger deeper into their hearts and relish it in secret. The anger of these people does not mitigate in time, but continues to brood within them.

Other people restrain their feelings of anger, because they have no opportunity for revenge. Their plight is unfortunate. "For wrath that is nursed in the heart, although it may not injure men who stand by, yet excludes the splendor of the radiance of the Holy Ghost, equally with wrath that is openly manifested (Ch XII).

Reminding us that the Lord does not permit us "to offer the spiritual sacrifices of our prayers" if we know that our brother has anything against us, Cassian interprets this as meaning that we cannot harbor anger for an instant, because the Apostle commands us to pray without ceasing and we cannot do that if we have anger within (Ch XIII).

Since even the old law of the Old Testament condemns anger, Cassian insists that the Healer of our souls, the Holy Spirit, wants us to eliminate all opportunities for anger and be reconciled with our brothers and sisters in Christ without delay. If we do become angry, we must accept responsibility for this sin and not lay the blame for our impatience and anger on other people, because unless we blame ourselves we will never learn to control our impatience and anger. We have control only over ourselves and we cannot make our spiritual progress and peace of mind depend on the will of another person (Ch XVII). As we accept responsibility for our anger and master it, we can enter into the contemplation of the deep mysteries of God.

Concluding his treatment of anger with suggestions as to how to deal with it according to the gospels, Cassian observes, "we ought not only to banish it from our actions, but entirely to root it out from our inmost soul" (Ch XX). Only by so doing will we be able to attain to the reward that is promised in the beatitude: "Blessed are the clean in heart for they shall see God" (Mt 5: 8). We are to "destroy the roots of our fault rather than the fruits" (Ch XX). To be victorious over anger, Cassian and the monks whose teaching he relays, believe that we should resolve never to tolerate anger in our hearts for any reason "because if the main light of our heart has been darkened by its shadows," "the purity of our soul will presently be clouded, and that it cannot possibly be made a temple for the Holy Ghost while the spirit of anger resides in us" (Ch XXXI). This is so important in his thinking that his closing thought on anger is that we should never pray or pour out our hearts to God while we are angry.

Thomas Aquinas takes a somewhat different approach to dealing with anger. Defining anger as a passion and a desire for revenge, Aquinas finds that "it is praiseworthy to desire vengeance as a corrective of vice and for the good of justice" (II 158). Such anger, termed "zealous anger" is desired according to the dictates of reason. However if one desires revenge contrary to reason by punishing someone who is innocent, or beyond what he deserves, and not for the correction of faults and upholding of law, such anger must be termed "sinful anger." However, zealous anger can also be sinful if it is "immoderately fierce" and causes one to depart from the love of God and neighbor and must be regarded as a grievous or mortal sin (II 158).

In evaluating the moral culpability of anger, Aquinas notes that there are two basic types of people who have long lasting anger, those that are "sullen" and those that he considers to be "ill-tempered" or "stern." The former, the sullen, keeps his anger shut up within himself for a long period of time not letting it break forth; eventually such anger slowly dissipates. By contrast, the anger in the so-called "ill-tempered" does not dissipate and can be satisfied only with revenge.

As we noted St. John Cassian, following the tradition of the desert fathers, believes that we should root out all anger from our souls to keep them in perfect peace as fitting temples of the Holy Spirit. St. Thomas, on the other hand, comments: "He that is without anger when he ought to be angry [just cause], imitates God as to lack of passion, but not as to God's punishing by judgment." Unless we are required to meet out punishment by virtue of our position in relation to the offender, it would seem to be more virtuous to refrain from judgment and to keep our souls free from anger in the peace of Christ who tells us: "Judge not, that you may not be judged" (Mt 7:1). St Paul offers similar counsel: "Revenge not yourselves, my dearly beloved; but give place unto wrath, for it is written: Revenge is mine, I will repay, says the Lord" (Rom 12: 19).

Turning from the dogmatic theology of St. Thomas Aquinas, we will now consider the ascetical theology of Adolphe Tanquerey S.S., who makes the observation that the struggle to conquer anger requires mortification that will purify the soul and prevent it from relapsing. In his justly famous book *The Spiritual Life*, he approaches anger in a tripartite manner–the nature, malice, and remedies of anger (407). He defines anger in this way: "Anger considered as a *passion* is a violent need of reaction caused by physical or moral suffering or annoyance. This vexation excites a violent emotion, which arouses our energies to overcome the difficulty. We are then prone to vent our anger upon persons, animals, and things" (407). He divides anger into two basic types, which he labels "red rage" and "white rage." With red rage the body responds with rapid breathing, pounding heart, reddened face, bulging eyes, flared nostrils, and the person experiencing the anger is ready to charge his adversary. In the case of white anger, breathing becomes difficult, the face become pale, cold sweat emerges on the brow and, with jaws tightly clenched, the person remains menacingly silent.

When anger is considered as a sentiment it "consists in a vehement desire to repel and punish an aggressor" (408). It is morally justifiable, according to Tanquerey, to have righteous indignation and to desire to seek retribution. Such was the anger of Jesus when he cleansed the temple of the money changers. To qualify as ethically good, righteous indignation must be just, tempered, and animated by sentiments of charity, otherwise there is moral guilt.

When anger is violent and has an excessive desire to inflict punishment it is considered a grievous sin. Often times such anger is accompanied with hatred that desires revenge. Tanquerey notes that there are degrees of intensity in anger or stages of the development of anger. They are (1) impatience; (2) display of temper; (3) agitation; (4) violence in words or blows; (5) fury or temporary insanity; and (6) ruthless hatred. To determine how sinful one's anger is, it is necessary to determine its intensity.

If our anger is simply just a *"transient impulse of passion,"* it is not a serious sin. However, if one loses self-control and the virtue of charity is seriously violated, a sin of passion can become grievous. If anger is rancorous and hateful, it qualifies as a serous sin when it is deliberate and done through an act of the will (409).

From the point of view of progress in the spiritual life, anger is a great impediment. Tanquerey, citing St. Gregory the Great, lists the harm unchecked anger does to the soul that wants to find freedom in God. It makes one lose (1) right judgment; (2) gentleness; (3) a feeling for justice; and (4) interior recollection. In sum, it interferes greatly with our union with God, destroys our peace of soul, and impedes our receiving grace (409).

Having demonstrated the devastating effects of anger, Tanquerey discusses remedies. We must, he insists "make use of every means at our disposal in order to over come the passion of anger" (410). First he suggests some physical means of assuaging the passion of anger—cool baths, proper food, and no alcoholic beverages. He suggests what he calls "moral hygiene" to combat anger. By this he means that we should always reflect before we speak, stamp out the first stirrings of anger, think about something else, and ask for God's help in allaying it, relying on His love to root out hatred, rancor, and vengeance (410).

We shall now consider conquering anger by reverting to what we have said in previous chapters of this book on eliminating fear and suffering from our lives. Since anger is the result of frustration, we realize that lying at the root of it are often our old enemies—desires, dependencies, and expectations. We make rules and when someone breaks one of them, we are frustrated and resentful and tempted to anger. For example, a family member spills red wine on our white carpet. Or perhaps the phone rings when we are in the middle of dinner. When we are deprived of things or people that we depend upon, we feel frustration and incipient anger. Our desires are thwarted and we become impatient. The degree of our anger will depend on how much we desire something and feel that we have to have it. If it is a minor consideration, perhaps we will feel only impatience. If we are undisciplined, our dissatisfaction can take on more obvious signs of our displeasure. We read of people on the highways caught up in road rage to the degree that they actually take a gun and kill the offending party.

Obviously, to conquer anger and the impatience that is its precursor, we have to get rid of desires and their dependencies. We have to disregard our expectations that things will be just the way we want them to be. They never are. As we become mature people, we realize this and make allowances for it and lower our expectations so that they conform to reality. When things turn out to be better than we hope for, we thank God and enjoy our good fortune. If someone spills red wine on our white carpet, we realize that it is not the end of the world, that in the long-range scheme of life, it is really inconsequential. It comes down to understanding that people are more important than sin.

Let us find freedom from anger, by realizing that most things that happen are not worth destroying our peace of soul by getting angry about them. However, do not pray for patience, as many people do. It has been our experience that when we pray for patience, the Lord gives us more opportunities to practice the virtue of patience. Daily life provides most of us with enough opportunities to practice patience without requesting the Lord to give us more.

We have to decide to live free from anger. It is a decision we have to make. Having made it, we eliminate all our dependencies and make our expectations conform to reality. If we have a houseful of children, things will get spilled on the carpet and we expect it to happen and will not let it disturb our peace when it does.

The rewards for living free from anger are great. The first and foremost is coming into closer union with God who loves to dwell with us and bestow His favors on a peaceful and tranquil soul. The harmony that will fill our lives and homes once we are free from anger will bless us and all those around us.

"Holy Spirit, we ask you to guide us in living lives free from anger and the turmoil it brings. Help us to realize that the events of daily life are not worth a single sin of anger. Fill our souls with charity toward all we encounter. With your wisdom, help us to diffuse the situations in our lives that tend to become inflammatory.

"Lord, Jesus, we receive your gift of peace. We know that no one can take it away from us. Only our thoughts and actions can rob us of your peace in our souls. We treasure your gift of peace and will guard it faithfully against anything that would tend to take us from it.

"Heavenly Father, we praise you and give you glory that with Your holy Wisdom we can live lives of happiness and joy free from anger. Amen."

Be Free From Food Addiction

A very common problem in our society today is obesity. If we just take a look around in public places, we see people who are grossly overweight. What is the problem and what can we do about it? One of the main causes of this serious problem is the size of portions. Restaurants serve much larger portions than formerly. One pound hamburgers are found on menus in fast food establishments together with extra sized fries and pints of sweetened beverages. Upscale restaurants serve gargantuan portions and because the food is on the plate it is consumed. Our culture has taught us to expect three meals a day, even if our bodies only require two. We eat because the clock on the wall says it is time for dinner when we are not hungry. We eat because we are bored. We eat because we feel sorry for ourselves and reward ourselves with treats. We stuff ourselves and our children with junk food that has nothing but empty calories. People try one diet after another, perhaps shedding a few pounds and then regaining them and even adding a few more when they go off the diet. What is the answer?

Turning now to the writing of St. John Cassian, we learn much about controlling the pleasures of the palate. This author warns against severe fasting, or dieting as it is mostly referred to today in our society, for it is often accompanied by relaxation afterwards that in turn leads to gluttony (*Institutes* Book 5 Ch IX). It is far better to eat moderately every day, than to withhold food for long fasts periodically. To overcome gluttonous desires, Cassian counsels us to join vigils, times of prayer, and holy reading to our fasting. One should consider the preparation of food to be a burden and to be a necessity for the body and not a source of pleasure (Ch XIV). By raising the mind to heavenly things, one can overcome the desire for food (Ch XV). According to Cassian, the basis of all spiritual battles must be based on the struggle against gluttony (Ch XVII). In effect, what he is saying is that we cannot win spiritual battles if we do not first subject our flesh and its desires, by controlling what we eat.

How then is one to proceed with taming the palate? According to Cassian, one must not eat between meals and one must also avoid delicacies. What are the benefits of taming the palate? He explains: "We shall have no external enemy to fear, if what is within is overcome and subdued to the spirit" (Ch XXI).

Defining gluttony as "the abuse of that legitimate pleasure God has attached to eating and drinking," Tanquerey observes that trouble arises when we make eating and drinking ends in themselves for enjoyment or in excessively consuming more than we need, even to the point of ruining our health, or causing drunkenness (411). He cites four different way in which we sin by gluttony; they are: (1) eating when we do not need to; (2) eating delicacies and gourmet food; (3) excessively eating and drinking to the point of injuring our health; and (4) eating in a greedy manner like an animal.

Tanquerey, believes as did Cassian, that the evil of gluttony is that it makes the soul a slave to the body, weakening one's intellectual and spiritual faculties, and therefore leading to a weakening of the moral life. He considers gluttony a grievous evil, if it makes it impossible for us to do our duties, or if it costs more than we can afford, or if it causes us to break the Church's laws of fast and abstinence. It is also a grievous fault if it is the cause of other serious sins. However, if one does not fall into inordinate excess, overindulgence is simply a venial sin.

Anyone who wants to make progress in the spiritual life must avoid gluttony, because it is a serious impediment to growing closer to God, even if it is only venially sinful because, Tanquerey insists, it weakens the will and encourages sensual pleasure and leads to dissipation (413).

To remedy gluttony, Tanquerey suggests that we recall that the pleasures of eating and drinking are means of sustaining our lives, not ends in themselves. He further explains: "Faith, however, tells us that the pleasures of eating and drinking must be sanctified by purity of intention, moderation and mortification" (413). He recommends that we should take the advice of St. Paul that whatever we eat or drink, we do it all to the glory of God.

We will now set forth our suggestions on how to overcome gluttony and be set free from food addiction. The problems we face with overeating are dealt with by curbing our desires that create dependencies and by changing our expectations. Having permitted our desires to create dependencies, we cannot resist chocolate cake, or perhaps donuts, or perhaps two glasses of Chardonnay with dinner. We expect to consume these things and if they are not available, we are disturbed because we have come to depend on them. They meet our expectations. Also we expect to eat certain foods and beverages at certain times. Perhaps we have become dependent on a glass of beer and a cheese sandwich at bedtime. If our expectations are not met, and our cravings for the things we are dependent upon are not satisfied, we become unpleasant to live with. If something disappointing happens, we try to bolster our morale by treating ourselves to something special——perhaps a candy bar. Whenever we get together with friends, we have to eat and drink. When we go to the cinema we have to eat. Football games? More food. We should not eat if we are not hungry.

To be free from our food addictions, we must seriously curb our dependencies, and we should look into our emotions. Every addiction speaks of an emotion that we cannot handle. If we address the deeper emotional reason for the cravings we experience, we will be able to manage them. Substituting something else for the thing we crave is a step in the right direction. In time, the cravings will pass. Furthermore, if we remove junk food and food with empty calories from our diet our cravings will lessen, because we are obtaining the nutrition our bodies need. If we give our bodies the vitamins and minerals they require, they will be satisfied and we will not feel the need to keep eating compulsively.

Quality of food is important, but quantity is also a factor in good nutrition. As a nation we are becoming addicted to larger portions of fries and bigger burgers. Consequently, we are rearing a generation of overweight children who have become accustomed to eating constantly.

To be fully satisfied, we need to receive spiritual nutrition as we eliminate our expectations and dependencies. We recommend the food of the angels, which according to St. John Damascene is God. This food we receive in three ways: (1) by reading the Word of God and (2) by private prayer; and (3) by partaking of the Body and Blood of Christ in the Holy Eucharist.

We recommend reading the Holy Scripture on a daily basis. A good place to begin, for those who have not developed the practice, is with the gospel of Mark, the shortest of the accounts of the good news of Jesus Christ. After that, perhaps the gospel of Luke with its accounts of the nativity should be read next. Then we would suggest the Acts of the Apostles that tells about the early history of the Church. The Psalter, the prayer book of the Church, can be our source of nourishment at anytime. After one has become comfortable with these reading, one might proceed to the epistles or letters that St Paul wrote to the churches. If one likes challenging thought, one might try the epistle to the Romans.

It is necessary to find a version of the Bible in modern English that can be easily read and understood. *The Jerusalem Bible* would be a nice choice. No matter which version is selected, we must nourish ourselves daily on the Word of God.

Prayer must be an important part of our lives, if we are to be set free from food addiction. To pray well, we need to learn about prayer. There is a lot more to prayer than reciting the vocal prayers we learned as children. As we advance in the spiritual life, we need to practice mental prayer and contemplation. The daily Bible reading should provide the material for mental prayer. We take the scripture reading and try to imagine we are there. Perhaps the reading for the day is one of the events in the life of our Lord, such as his birth in Bethlehem. We imagine the animals that are crowded around the manger scene. We notice the joy on the face of Mary as she smiles down at the newborn baby. Next, we consider St. Joseph and the shepherds. Exploring the scene as long as we wish, perhaps we even reach down and touch one of His baby feet and maybe even kiss it. We conclude by praising the Heavenly Father for sending us His son and whispering to the sleeping baby that we love Him. Mental prayer can be as simple as that.

Contemplative prayer can even be simpler. Simply gazing in wonder at the babe in the manger, we open our hearts to receive Him and embrace Him in love.

When trying to control our expectations for too much food and eliminate the dependencies we have for certain foods that our desires have created, we need to turn to the Living Bread, the Body and Blood of Christ for help. Here is what Jesus tells us about this:

> Then Jesus said to them: Amen, amen I say unto you. Except you eat the flesh of the Son of man, and drink His blood, you shall not have life in you. He that eats my flesh, and drinks my blood, has everlasting life: and I will raise him up in the last day. For my flesh is meat indeed: and my blood is drink indeed.
>
> He that eats my flesh, and drinks my blood, abides in me, and I in him. (Jn 6: 54–6: 58)

Nothing can be much clearer than this statement that His flesh is meat indeed and His blood is drink indeed and He dwells in us when we partake of them. However, we must partake in a worthy manner. St. Paul cautions us that if we do not, we drink damnation to ourselves, because we do not discern the body of the Lord. The Apostle adds to this cautionary statement the following: "Therefore are there many infirm and weak among you, and many sleep" (1 Cor 11: 27–29). Because such people fail to perceive that Jesus, Body and Blood and Soul and Divinity, is really and truly present within them when they receive the Eucharist, they do not experience a healing encounter with Him, and for this reason many of them are sick. They missed the time of their visitation.

In the New Testament, Jesus continually heals those who encounter Him and wish to be healed. His Presence is always a healing presence. But if we do not recognize that He is present with us, we cannot receive our healing. We must touch Him with our faith. When we do this He will heal us. If our faith is weak, receiving Him worthily will strengthen the theological virtues of faith, hope and love within us. When we receive Him in communion, we need to ask Him to heal us of our addictions to our daily bread and give us a desire to partake of the Living Bread.

If we overindulge in food because of our expectations that a hearty meal will be on the table with more than we need or because we partake of foods that we are addicted to because of our dependencies, we should confess this, even though it is most likely a venial sin at most. If we eat so much that it is damaging to our health, then it can be a grievous sin and must be confessed, as should be the over-indulgence in alcoholic beverages.

Food addiction can be overcome by following the suggestions we have given. People have a tendency to keep eating and drinking the same things day in and day out. One can break dependencies by substituting something else in place of the desired food or beverage. By feeding one's soul with the Word of God, prayer, and the sacraments one can be set free from food addictions and live a happier life without the encumbrances–both spiritual and physical of obesity.

"Lord, we ask you to help us learn to control our appetite for food. We want to keep our bodies well and healthy so they may be beautiful temples for your indwelling Presence. May we learn to eat those things that are good for us and avoid the things that make us fat and ugly. Strengthen our wills so that we may control what we eat, for we know that a strong spiritual life is based on self-con-trol. Amen."

Be free from Turmoil!

Life is fraught with turmoil. Sleeping pills, tranquilizers, drugs, and alcohol are the things many people employ to try to find refuge from their anxieties. The highest cause of death among young people is suicide. Our cities are filled with crime to such a degree that it is unsafe to go out on the streets at night. Murders, robberies, and mayhem are the headlines that scream out at us from the daily newspapers. Yet, the Holy Scripture tells us: "God will bless His people with peace" (Ps 28:10). The God of peace will be with you.

Peace in the streets of our cities, peace among nations, peace between races is the prophetic announcement of the Messiah's presence among us. The people who love God should be the ones who make sure His presence is felt throughout the world by becoming peacemakers. Peace comes from reconciliation with God and with our neighbors. Jesus comes bringing peace for the whole world, but to find this peace we must be reconciled with all. It seems impossible that everyone could live in peace, but we know that all is possible with God.

In order to have peace, there must be justice in society. Where there is sin and injustice, there can be no peace. Jesus tells us, "Blessed are the peacemakers for they shall be called the children of God" (Mt 5: 9).

Jesus has the answer for every life and every person. No one who comes to Jesus Christ ever leaves with empty hands. There are answers for us all in the name of Christ Jesus. There *are* solutions to our problems. There *is* hope. This does not mean that we will have no problems, but rather that our problems will be turned into blessings. We do not know what the future holds, but we do know that God has a plan of justice and perfection, salvation and joy for our lives. If we abandon ourselves into His hands, He will show us the way to happiness and peace. We must live in the name of Jesus and in His presence. If we do this, He will transform us from glory to glory, until we reflect His perfect image and our hearts are filled with His peace.

It is an obvious fact that when a ship is overloaded, it can easily sink. If we carry a lot of excess baggage in our souls, they too can sink. We need to get rid of all the things that weigh heavily upon our spirits. These include bitterness, envy, hatred, sadness, pessimism, self-pity, and depression, among other things. If we want our souls to sail like sturdy ships and be free from turmoil, we must eliminate such negative forces from our lives.

Jesus is much stronger than our sadness and more powerful than all our problems. Many people go through life complaining about their problems, but do nothing to resolve them. The first step in finding peace and living free from turmoil is achieved when we rise up, rejoice, and put all our concerns in the hands of the Savior. St Paul insists emphatically: "And we know that to them that love God, all things work together unto good, to such as, according to his purpose, are called to be saints" (Rom 8: 28). And that includes all of us. We are all called to be saints.

Although nothing seems to be going right in our lives and it seems that we are headed for disaster, we will proclaim that everything is for the good for those who love God. Another verse of Holy Scripture that we stand on is: "I can do all these things in Him who strengthens me" (Phil 4: 13). When things are difficult, we acknowledge that if we do not have obstacles, we will not have victory, knowing that Christ will give us the victory in every part of life. We know that tomorrow will be better than today, because our God and King is already present in tomorrow just waiting for us to catch up to Him.

We have no need to know the future; we shun such things as horoscopes. Our star is the radiant morning star, Jesus Christ, who can do all things and who supplies us with joy, answers, and the right perspective on life. So let us empty our hearts of all negative feelings—guilt, sadness, hatred, envy, and the like. Let us tell the Lord that we want to live peaceful victorious lives free from all turmoil. Let us make our lives a song of praise that glorifies God.

Since God has given His Son for us to suffer and to die, will He not give us all the other things we need too? (Rom 8: 32). Jesus did not come into the world to condemn the world but to save it. As St. Paul explains: "There is therefore now no condemnation to them which are in Christ Jesus, who walk not after the flesh, but after the Spirit" (Rom 8: 1).

Far too many of us are in slavery to our desires, our sins, and our emotions. Chains that seem impossible to break bind us. However, Jesus, the liberator and redeemer of all people, the power of the Father incarnate, can break all the chains that keep us in turmoil. He can bring justice and salvation. In Christ, we are more than conquerors. We can have victory over alcohol, illicit sex, divorce, sickness and disease, and other ills, if we let Him lead us to the Father.

Everyone who draws near to Jesus Christ enters into a relationship with the Heavenly Father. We can see this very plainly in the conversation Jesus has with the Apostle Philip. Philip says unto him, "Lord, show us the Father, and it suffices us." Jesus replies:

> "Have I been so long a time with you, and yet have you not known me, Philip? He that has seen me has seen the Father; and how do you say then, 'Show us the Father?' Do you not believe that I am in the Father, and the Father in me? The words that I speak unto you I speak not of myself, but the Father that dwells in me, he does the works. Believe me that I am in the Father, and the Father in me, or else believe me for the very works' sake." (Jn 4: 8–11)

Sometimes we seem to be as confused as Philip and fail to understand that everything Jesus does is related to the Father. We make the sign of the cross, blessing ourselves in the name of the Father, the Son, and the Holy Spirit, but we often lack understanding about the Trinity to whom our entire lives are directed. We are on our way to the Father, through Jesus Christ, in union with the Holy Spirit. We are all pilgrims on our way to the Father who has prepared eternal mansions for us in glory. All of life is the way to God. All benediction of the Father resides in Jesus Christ. If we know Jesus, we know the Father. And if we know the Father, we have eternal life. "This is life eternal life that they might know You, the only true God, and Jesus Christ, whom You have sent" (Jn 17: 3). If we know the Father and Jesus, we already have eternal life. We are in it now and we shall never taste death; we shall cross through the valley of the shadow of death, but a shadow cannot destroy us.

How do we know Jesus Christ? We learn to know Him from reading the inspired Word of God that reveals Him to us. We know Him by receiving His pardon in the Sacrament of Reconciliation. We learn of Him in the Sacrament of the Healing of the Sick. We experience His love in the Holy Eucharist as we enfold Him in our souls.

We need a credible Church that is overflowing with love where everyone is welcome and feels that God loves him/her, because the members show love to each other. We are fully cognizant of the fact that we are the Church and we are ever striving to renew it. The Church is always in need of renewal because her members are human beings who do not foresee the consequences of their actions. Nevertheless, the Church is holy, spotless and without wrinkle because of the great holiness of the Mother of Jesus who is the prototype of the Church and its most perfect member whom we all emulate.

When we hunger for God, it shows that something wonderful is happening—that God is renewing His Church. It shows that people believe in Christ and are encountering the Father. The smiling faces of the people in the pews show that the Holy Spirit is present in His people. And when we pray something wonderful happens.

We believe in prayer, because Jesus tells plainly of its power:

> "Verily, verily, I say unto you, He that believes on me, the works that I do shall you do also, and greater works than these shall you do, because I go unto my Father. And whatsoever you shall ask in my name, that will I do, that the Father may be glorified in the Son." (Jn 14: 12–13)

Do we believe this? Are we putting it into practice? If we believe that Christ will give us what we ask for in his Name, He will. When He is present with us in the Eucharist, it is an excellent time to ask for what we need. It is an especially good time to ask Him for healing, for He is a healing Lord.

In the Scriptures, He is continually healing people who come into His presence. All masses are healing masses. Why then are more people not being healed? Simply because they do not ask for His healing touch, therefore they do not receive it. Not do they receive the peace that the blessings of the mass offers with the ancient "Pax Domini sit semper vobiscum," "May the peace of the Lord be always with you." Jesus is always present in our hearts to answer our prayers. We need to confide our lives into His loving hands and let Him guide us on the way to the Father. If we try to guide ourselves we make mistakes. He knows the way to the Father and He will guide us, if we let Him. He will fill our souls with His peace and free us from turmoil.

Asking the Father in Jesus name does not mean constantly repeating His name, but rather abandoning ourselves into His hands. When we do this, marvelous things happen in our lives. Our lives blossom and bear fruit, when we conform them to His plan for our happiness.

Jesus says if we love Him, we will keep His commandments. It is impossible to understand Christian morality, if we do not love Him. When we understand what the love of Jesus signifies, we give up sin. Those who love Him really do keep His commandments. When we come to understand what the pardon of our sins means and how He purchased our pardon with His cross and resurrection, we begin to comprehend His great love.

Most amazing of all, while we were still sinners, Christ died for us (Rom 5: 8). God loves us, just as we are, with our sins. His love is much greater than our debility and our sins. When we come to understand the love of Jesus Christ, we know that God accepts us as we are. Jesus tells each one of us: "Behold, I stand at the gate, and knock. If any man shall hear my voice, and open to me the door, I will come in to him, and will sup with him, and he with me" (Rom 3: 20). We have to open the door, if we want Him to enter. Jesus even promises to bring the Father with Him:

> "If any one loves me, he will keep my word, and my Father will love him, and we will come to him, and will make our abode with him. He that loves me not, keeps not my words. And the word, which you have heard, is not mine; but the Father's who sent me." (Jn 14: 23–24)

Jesus is not speaking in a figurative manner in saying that He and the Father will make their abode with us. He really means it and people down through the centuries in all ages of the Church have experienced His presence mystically within. Speaking of himself and his prayer, St. Alphonsus Rodriguez wrote:

> And, at once he was lifted up above all created things. He found himself as it were in another region, alone with God, who gave him great light concerning the knowledge of God and of self. His knowledge of God, which was without intermediary and reasoning and, consequently, his love for God and his intimate familiarity with Him, rose to such a pitch that it seemed as if the Almighty desired to make Himself known to him as he does to the Blessed in heaven. O heavenly banquet! God invites the soul, and in this banquet of love He giveth Himself! O supreme love! O heavenly love! O precious love. The soul forgets all earthly things and forgets her own self also, because she is solely occupied in loving God, who is so intimately present to her. (Poulain 268–269)

When we feel the Divine Love coursing through our being, we know for a certainty that God loves us. We know that it is Love that framed the heavens and keeps the stars speeding through the sky. The whole universe is awash with love. We all need to feel loved by God. Some are tortured because they do not feel loved by God. Many think their sins are greater than the love of God. Still others feel that they are not worthy of God's love. They need to understand that God loves us just as we are—mediocre, limited sinners.

The very first thing we must learn as Christians is that God loves us. We are His beloved children. The love of God is a cataract that envelops, transforms, and guides us. When we feel loved, all is beautiful and wondrous. We are filled with peace.

So that we might live in the peace of God, Jesus promised to send us the Holy Spirit. Where God is, there is love. Where He has been, there is peace. Jesus sends us the Spirit of Truth to remind us of all He has told us. The world cannot receive His Spirit; it does not know Him. Jesus sends Him to us to lead us into all truth. If we open our hearts to Him, the Holy Spirit will descend upon us, enter our souls, and bring with Him His peace. He will open our eyes so that we see clearly. He reveals His presence and the mystery of God to us. He shows us what pardon and the love of God mean. He invites us to reconciliation. We have to have very hard hearts not to respond to God's merciful love when He tells us that this is the time of mercy and pardon. From the Holy Spirit we learn: "Nor height, nor depth, nor any other creature, shall be able to separate us from the love of God, which is in Christ Jesus our Lord" (Rom 8: 38–39).

Finally, in order to be free from turmoil we have to simplify our lives. We get involved in so many projects and plans that we feel pressured trying to accomplish them all. For the love and peace of God, we must simplify our lives as much as possible.

Peace is a great gift from Jesus to each one of us. It was His parting gift as He prepared to return to His Father. "Peace I leave with you, my peace I give unto you; not as the world gives, do I give unto you. Let not your heart be troubled, nor let it be afraid (John 14: 27). We must receive His gift of peace. If we do, our hearts will not be troubled or afraid. We need to receive His gift of peace daily each morning. Then throughout the day we must guard the peace that He has placed in our hearts and not let anyone rob us of it. We have control over our thoughts. If anyone tries to make us feel anxious or troubled, we must reject these thoughts immediately. To do this, we can recite a verse of Holy Scripture reminding us of the peace of Christ.

We can recall for example His words quoted above and receive them as our own, thanking Him for His gift of peace. Or perhaps another verse such as, "Let not your hearts be troubled, you believe in God, believe also in Me." The God of peace will be with us.

"Lord Jesus we thank you for your gift of peace. We will guard it in our souls and not let anyone steal it from us. We praise You, Lord, that You have loved us so much that You pour your love and peace into our souls, uniting us closely to You, the Heavenly Father, and the Holy Spirit. Amen."

Be Free of Deception

Self-deception is one of the main causes of our unhappiness. We do not perceive reality as it is, but rather are caught up in a web of delusion, trapped by our inability to perceive the truth. To keep from deception, we need to know the difference between our desires and our necessities. To keep from living disillusioned and frustrated lives we need to know exactly what our necessities are and separate them from our desires.

One of the greatest illusions we hold is that some person or some possession will make us happy. Happiness comes from Jesus Christ alone. No human being can grant us inner peace or joy for a very long time. Such happiness is reserved for those who understand the meaning of God's plan in this life and in the life of the world to come.

Often the reason our relationships fail in the present life is that we do not perceive the person as God actually sees him/her. We fantasize about him/her imagining the one we love to be a certain way, in short, to be a phantasm. When we learn what the person is really like, love shrivels and dies. We can avoid this if we learn to love unconditionally, particularly when we ask the Lord to teach us to see the person with His sight, His purpose, and His meaning. We also need to realize that, if we cannot be happy in ourselves, no one can make us happy.

To be free from deception, we need drastically to change the basic orientation of our lives. We must give up the values and ideas of the culture in which we live and orient ourselves toward the values of the Holy Trinity, eliminating the deceitful desires that corrupt us (Eph 4: 22). We must be renewed in the spirit of our minds and recreated in justice and holiness (Eph 4: 24). We must become new creatures and this means dying to the desires of the flesh that deceive us and lead us away from God.

How easily we fall into deception. We desire riches, but they are not necessary for our happiness. We do need to have enough wealth to provide the necessities of life. God will grant each of us whatever is needed for our mission in life and enough money to cover our needs and do good works to help others. In fact, we must ardently desire to realize our mission, but not covet wealth. Desire of other people's wealth will lead us to frustration and envy, and that will only be a cause of suffering. We should want what God wishes us to have no more or no less.

Perhaps until now, we have been trying to attain to and experience the goals of our culture that keep urging us to more and more consumerism. We find life tedious and wearisome as we chase after more and more material possessions, until finally we learn that they do not make us happy. If we want to be free of deception, we must banish anger, envy, pride, and gluttony from our hearts and lives. The Holy Scripture warns us: "Beware lest perhaps your heart be deceived, and you depart from the Lord, and serve strange gods, and adore them" (De 11: 16). If we are possessed by deceptive desires, we can never be satisfied. "And as wine deceives him that drinks it, so shall the proud man be, and he shall not be honored who has enlarged his desire like hell and is himself like death, and he is never satisfied" (Hab 2: 5).

There are two outstanding cases of self-deception in the New Testament. All those involved are healed by Jesus of their deception and are then able to perceive reality clearly. When Mary Magdalene goes to the tomb on Easter morning, she sees Jesus there and thinks He is the gardener, until He heals her deception by calling her by name. The disciples on the road to Emmaus Easter Sunday night do not realize that it is Jesus who walks down the road with them and comes into their home. Only when He takes bread and blesses it, when He celebrates the Holy Eucharist, do they recognize Him in the breaking of the bread, as He opens their eyes to reality. Jesus wants to heal us of our deceptions as well. He wants us to be happy and to share His glory in the life of the world to come. Happiness comes from Jesus Christ, but we must renounce and reject our love of sadness, just as Mary Magdalene had to reject and renounce her sadness before she was able to perceive reality and see Jesus. The disciples of Emmaus also had to reject their sadness and their deception that the Messiah had not yet come, before they were able to see Jesus in the breaking of the bread.

Jesus Himself cautions us against being deceived: "Take heed lest any man deceive you" (Mk 13: 5). St. Paul cautions us likewise against deception. "Let no man deceive himself; if any man among you seems to be wise in this world, let him become a fool, that he may be wise" (1Co 3: 18). True wisdom comes from God and is a gift of the Holy Spirit that is given to us when we ask for it. Warning us against pride, St. Paul says we deceive ourselves when we have too high an opinion of ourselves. "For if any man thinks himself to be something, whereas he is nothing, he deceives himself" (Gal 6: 3). In this case, it is our pride that causes us to be deceived. He calls us to come out of the darkness into the light of Christ.

"For you were heretofore darkness, but now light in the Lord. Walk then as children of the light" (Eph 5: 8).

Another form of deception that can overtake us comes when we do not recognize our own sins. The beloved St. John writes: "If we say we have no sin, we deceive ourselves, and the truth is not in us" (1Jn 1: 8). This deception appears to be very prevalent nowadays as relatively few people find their way into the confessional. Sin separates us from God and is the root cause of our unhappiness. St. John tells us that if we walk in the darkness of deception, we do not really know Him. If we walk in the light, His light, His blood cleanses us from all our sins, and if we confess them, He faithfully forgives us our sins and cleanses us from all unrighteousness. However, if we say we have not sinned, God's word is not in us and we are calling Him a liar (1 Jn 1: 69).

Furthermore, St. John advises us that we are not to love the things of the world, because if we do, the love of the Heavenly Father is not in us. "For all that is in the world, the lust of the flesh, and the lust of the eyes, and the pride of life, is not of the Father, but is of the world. And the world passes away and the lust thereof, but he that does the will of God abides forever" (1 Jn 2: 16–17). Finally, St. John explains that we can tell who the children of God are and who the children of the devil are: "In this the children of God are manifest, and the children of the devil; whosoever does not righteousness is not of God, neither he that loves not his brother" (1 Jn 3: 10). The children of God love their brothers and sisters in Christ and avoid every unrighteous act.

If we are truly sincere about getting rid of our deceptions, we need to search our souls, confess our sins, and work hard to amend our lives. It does not do us much good to go to confession and not have a determined intention to improve ourselves by avoiding in the future the sins we confess. If we are resolute in our decision to get sin and the deception it brings out of our lives, we will receive enough sacramental grace to conquer our sins and free ourselves from deception. We need to examine our consciences as to whether the roots of the seven capital sins are entrenched in us, for they are the root of all sins we commit.

One of the most deceptive desires of the human heart is the desire for fame. We all do desire fame, but fame is fleeting. We do need some of it, but we need to realize that fame never last very long and is not worth losing our peace of soul to acquire.

Some of us long for power, especially in the middle years of life. Perhaps this is due to our pride and our desire to dominate other people. We try to control family and friends, and others according to our position in life. Many are frustrated because they do not have the power they desire. The thirst for power is part of the human psyche, but the sooner we realize that the power we think we wield is unreal, the happier we will be, because no one really holds any power over anyone else. People may obey because of the circumstances, but not because they like it. The sooner we will find that true happiness comes only from Jesus Christ, the King of Glory, the better off we will be.

People of all ages, but particularly older ones, may find the sin of avarice or greed trying to dominate their lives. Older people seem to feel that their money and worldly possessions will bring them happiness and protect them from death. Let us avoid all avarice knowing that Jesus will provide every human being with an abundance that will cover all needs.

In addition to turning from false gods, such as pride, power, and greed, we must discipline ourselves. Without self-control and self-discipline we cannot rid ourselves of our deceptions, nor can Jesus heal us of them, until we take control of our lives.

To be free from deception we must know that no person or situation can rob us of the peace Jesus came to give us. We must open ourselves daily to receive His peace. Then we must guard it by controlling our thoughts, because only our own thoughts can rob us of His peace that passes all understanding.

Another form of deception comes from taking drugs or inordinately consuming alcoholic beverages. Not only do these intoxicants darken our minds when we are under their influence, making it difficult for us to perceive reality, they actually do damage to our bodies causing us to lose valuable cells in the brain, plus giving us many other physical problems. Anyone who wishes to avoid deception will exercise self-control in the use of alcoholic beverages and avoid all drugs.

Now is the day of salvation. Let us open our hearts now to the healing touch of Jesus Christ, asking Him to help us banish all deception from our lives.

"Lord Jesus, we want to be free from all deception. We want to see reality from your perspective. We reject all sadness and melancholy because we know they prevent us from seeing clearly. We know that the seven capital sins can cause us to be deceived; we will examine our souls for them and pull them out at their roots. We know that fame, power, and possessions cannot bring us happiness and that they are chimeras that deceive us and lead us away from You.

"Holy Spirit, lead us to Jesus. Lord Jesus, show us the way to the Father.

Heavenly Father we want to be your children, children of the Light, walking in your ways in truth. Amen."

Free from the Law of Sin and Death

We live in a dying world that is subject to destruction. Beautiful flowers wither and fade and are tossed out with the garbage. The lovely face of youth turns into wrinkles and old age unseemliness. Time is the destroyer, the grim reaper that steals life away. While we know in our hearts what is right and what we should do, we do not do it, and often do things we should not do. St. Paul shared these feelings and cried out, "Unhappy man that I am, who shall deliver me from the body of this death?" Immediately he answers his own question with these words: "The grace of God, by Jesus Christ our Lord. Therefore, I myself, with the mind serve the law of God; but with the flesh, the law of sin" (Rom 7: 24–25). If the apostle felt this division within his being between the law of God and sin, it is surely the state in which most Christians find themselves because of original sin brought upon us by our human nature.

The prophet Isaiah foretold that Messiah would come and "open the eyes of the blind, and bring forth the prisoner out of prison, and them that sit in darkness out of the prison house" (Is 42: 7). And when Christ came, He read this prophecy of Isaiah in the synagogue of Nazareth and said "This day is fulfilled this scripture in your ears" (Luke 4: 21).

We have been delivered from the power of darkness and brought into the kingdom of God's Son, our Lord Jesus Christ. Unfortunately, many of us just do not realize that yet and continue plodding along in the darkness of sin, instead of living in the glory of the liberty of the children of God. St. Paul, realizing keenly the division that exists in the human heart, pulling it toward and at the same time away from God, exclaimed, "the law of the spirit of life, in Christ Jesus, has delivered me from the law of sin and death" (Rom 8: 2). As a righteous Pharisee, Paul or Saul of Tarsus as he was called before his conversion to Christ, had tried diligently to keep the Law of Moses and found it to be extremely difficult to keep the entire law. In more recently times, it is told that Benjamin Franklin decided to practice virtue and ran into difficulties because he would make progress with one virtue only to discover that the other ones he had previously worked on suffered by neglect. If we try to climb to God by a ladder of good deeds, we soon discover that we go up three steps and fall back one or two or even three or more. We cannot climb to God by own efforts. We cannot lift ourselves up by our own bootstraps. This is what St. Paul experienced and wrote about so penetratingly in the book of Romans, coming up with this conclusion: "There is now therefore no condemnation to them that are in Christ Jesus, who walk not according to the flesh. For the law of the spirit of life, in Christ Jesus, hath delivered me from the law of sin and of death. (Rom 8: 1–2).

The good news is that God has adopted us as sons and daughters and has sent His Spirit into our hearts (Gal 4: 3–6). We have not received a spirit of bondage, but have become the adopted children of God and the Holy Spirit Himself bears witness to this (Rom 8: 15–16). Because of this adoption and the indwelling of the Spirit of God we are set free. As St. Paul says, "Where the Spirit of the Lord is, there is liberty" (2 Cor 3: 17).

Our Lord Himself promises liberty to His disciples. Speaking to the Jews who believed in Him, Jesus said: "If you continue in my word, you shall be my disciples indeed and you shall know the truth, and the truth shall make you free" (Jn 8: 31–32). When the Jews replied that they had never been slaves to anyone and asked Him to explain what he meant that they would be free, he said, "Amen, amen I say unto you that whosoever commits sin, is the servant of sin." Then he added, "If therefore the Son shall make you free, you shall be free indeed" (Jn 8: 36).

Christ sets us free from the law of sin and death so that we can serve Him in the Spirit. Filled with His Spirit, if we try to climb the ladder to God and start to fall, He will catch us in His everlasting arms and keep us from falling, for He has redeemed us from the curse of the law (Gal 3: 13). Furthermore, He has delivered us from a lifelong fear of death, for death holds no terrors for those Spirit filled people who live in Christ (Heb 2: 15). We are no longer slaves to sin, but have become servants of righteousness and justice (Rom 6: 18). We have, as St. Paul explains, been "delivered from the servitude of corruption, into the liberty of the glory of the children of God" (Rom 8: 21). For this reason, St. Paul says, "There is now therefore no condemnation to them that are in Christ Jesus, who walk not according to the flesh" (Rom 8: 1).

Unfortunately, there are many of us who hear the Word of God that is meant to set us free and do not do what the Word tells us. Such a person, according to the Apostle James, is like a man who looks at himself in a mirror and walks away and soon forgets what kind of man he is. "But he that has looked into the perfect law of liberty, and has continued in it, not becoming a forgetful hearer, but a doer of the work, this man shall be blessed in his deed" (Jas 1: 23–25). Having been set free from sin and having become the servants of God, we attain righteousness and everlasting life. We are the righteousness of God (2 Cor 5: 21). The wages of sin is death, but the gift of God is eternal life through our Lord Jesus Christ.

If we are in fellowship with Christ, we walk in the light of the Holy Spirit and do good. If we walk in darkness and obscurity and our deeds are evil, we are not telling the truth, if we say we belong to Christ. If we walk in the light as He is in the light—God is Light and there is no darkness in Him—and our deeds are good, we are in fellowship with Christ and His blood cleanses us from all sin.

It has often been said that the greatest sin of our twenty-first century is that we have lost the consciousness of sin. The sacrament of reconciliation is the most neglected sacrament in the Church today. Yet, at the mass on Sunday, vast crowds still flock to the communion rail to receive the Body and Blood of Christ. What about their sins? Do they deny having them? St. John in his first epistle writes: "If we say that we have no sin, we deceive ourselves, and the truth is not in us. If we confess our sins, He is faithful and just, to forgive us our sins, and to cleanse us from all iniquity. If we say that we have not sinned, we make Him a liar, and His word is not in us" (1 Jn 1: 8–10). The Apostle John explains that he is writing this epistle so that we in the Church may not sin, but if we do sin, he wants us to know that "we have an advocate with the Father, Jesus Christ the just, and He is the propitiation for our sins, and not for ours only, but also for those of the whole world" (1 Jn 2: 1–2). Because Jesus died on the cross to make us one with God, to bring atonement for our sins, and because He has risen from the dead and lives ever to make intercession for us before the throne of the eternal Father, He is our advocate or attorney propitiatorily.

John tells us quite plainly how to determine if we really know Christ or not. It is very easy to tell. If we know Him, we keep His commandments. If we say we know Him and do not keep His commandments, we are not telling the truth (1 Jn 2: 3–4). And what are His commandments? You shall love the Lord, your God with all your heart, all you mind, and with all your strength and love your brother as you love yourself. If we do not love our brothers and sisters in Christ, we are not abiding in Christ, His Spirit, and the truth and we walk in darkness. As John says, "he that hates his brother is in darkness, and walks in darkness, and knows not whither he goes, because the darkness has blinded his eyes" (1 Jn 2: 11). Those who are in Christ, John says, have an anointing from the Holy Spirit that leads us into all truth (1 Jn 2: 20).

Those who have been set free from the law of sin and death do not love the world or the things of the world that is decaying and passing away, rather, they strive to be holy as He is holy. John explains that we do not know what we shall become. "We know, that, when He shall appear, we shall be like to him, because we shall see him as He is. And everyone that has this hope in Him, sanctifies himself, as He also is holy" (1 Jn: 32–33). If we abide in Him, we will not sin, as John states: "Whosoever abides in Him, sins not; and whosoever sins, has not seen Him, nor known Him" (1 Jn 3: 6). This is what Jesus Himself told us. "By their fruits you shall know them. Do men gather grapes of thorns, or figs of thistles? Even so every good tree brings forth good fruit, and the evil tree brings forth evil fruit. A good tree cannot bring forth evil fruit; neither can an evil tree bring forth good fruit (Mt: 7: 16–18).

In addition to doing good deeds and loving our brothers and sisters in Christ, the manifestations of the Holy Spirit in our lives give testimony that we do abide in Christ and Christ in us. The Holy Spirit is made manifest in the gifts that He bestows on true believers, gifts of the Holy Spirit, enabling them to live and die, modeling the beatitudes and resplendent with happiness and joy. The prophet Isaiah lists the gifts of the Holy Spirit as being, in ascending order, the gifts of fear, piety, knowledge, fortitude, counsel, understanding, and wisdom (11: 2). When the Holy Spirit moves in us, we experience His presence as He manifests Himself to us and, in so doing, speaks to us of the plenitude of the revelation of Jesus Christ and the life of God in us. In addition to the gifts, the one who abides in Christ and lives in His Spirit can expect to receive charisms of the Holy Spirit. Some of the charisms are (1) speaking in tongues; (2) interpretation of tongues; (3) words of wisdom; (4) words of knowledge; (5) the working of miracles; (6) gifts of healing; (7) the gift of helps or helpers; and finally (8) the gift of prophecy. The Holy Spirit will give these charisms to believers, if they are open to receiving them and letting the Spirit work through them.

Because God has given us His Spirit we know that we abide in Him. Because we love one another, we know that we are His. Because we confess that Jesus is the Son of God and the Redeemer of the world, we know that He abides in us. As St. John says, we have come to know the love of God and when we abide in love we abide in God, and God in us. God's love is made perfect in us that we may have confidence in Him on the Day of Judgment.

When love is perfect, there will be no fear in us. "Fear is not in charity: but perfect charity casts out fear, because fear hath pain. And he that fears is not perfected in charity. Let us therefore love God, because God first loved us" (1 Jn 4: 18–19). Let us put aside all fear and strive to live in the Spirit.

We need to become better acquainted with the Holy Spirit who came together with the Eternal Father and Jesus Christ to dwell within us at our baptism. At confirmation, we received more of the Spirit of God, but some people still do not know Him. Perhaps they are even like the man in the Scripture that did not even know that there is a Holy Spirit. Perhaps this is because it is difficult to visualize Him. We can easily picture God the Son and God the Father, but the Holy Spirit has no human likeness to which one can relate Him. He is not a dove, although a dove at the baptism of Jesus symbolized him. Nor is He the wind, even though on the day of Pentecost, He was like a mighty rushing wind. He is a Spirit—not a force or a thing—and a Divine Person, the third Person of the Blessed and Eternal Trinity. He loves each of us with a personal love and is waiting for us to respond to His love reciprocally. Everyone who is filled with the Spirit of God is drawn by the Spirit into the life of the Trinity. If we open our hearts to Him, we will see the glory of God. He will begin to do wonderful things in and for us.

How do we grow in union with the Holy Spirit? A good way to begin is to invite Him into our lives, our hearts, and our homes. We can simply breathe a prayer saying, "Holy Spirit, we welcome you here." When we are tempted to do something that we know is not right, we can ask Him to keep us from yielding. If we do yield, we can immediately tell Him that we are sorry and ask for His forgiveness. When we need to make a decision about what we are going to do, we need to ask Him for His guidance, for He is our constant companion—nearer to us than breathing and closer than hands and feet—and we need to recognize His presence, thanking Him for His loving care of us. Every year we should make the novena to the Holy Spirit during the days before Pentecost. When Pentecost Sunday comes, we should celebrate it as the great feast of the Church that it is, remembering that when the Spirit was poured out on the Blessed Mother and the apostles in the Upper Room, He transformed fearful men into fearless champions of Christ who were ready to shed their blood for Him and His gospel. The Holy Spirit is Power. Just as He transformed the Apostles, He can transform us, making it easy with His grace to avoid sin and practice righteousness, integrity, and justice. He picks us up and carries us over the rough roads of life so that we no longer stumble and fall when we meet adversity or temptation. Instead we overcome; we are more than conquerors because of Him who loved us and sent us His Spirit to be our Comforter, Defender, and our Guide.

We are confident in the face of all adversity because nothing, absolutely nothing, can separate us from the love of God that is in Christ, His Holy Spirit, and the Eternal Father. Nothing in this life or in death can sever us from Their exceedingly great love.

"Lord, Jesus, we thank you for dying for us to redeem us and for sending us your Holy Spirit to be our constant companion in this life and in the world to come. We welcome you, Sweet Spirit of Love. Fill our hearts, our lives, and our homes with Your presence. Guide us, direct us and be our comfort in the trials of this world so that we may be in the world, but not of the world, as Jesus prayed we might be. Teach us to turn to you with all our problems. Be health for our minds and bodies. Be our strength when we are troubled and harassed by difficulties. Be our joy even in the midst of trials and pain. Dear Sweet Spirit, take us always to Jesus so that He may lead us to the Heavenly Father. And You Eternal Father, we thank you for Your great love that sent us Jesus. We are thankful that You so loved the world that You gave Your only begotten Son that whoever believes in Him might not perish, but have eternal life. We thank you, Wonderful Father, that you sent us the Holy Spirit, the Paraclete, to be our help on the way to You. Holy Trinity, One God in Three Divine Persons, we adore you, we praise, we give you thanks for Your great glory. Amen."

The Freedom of the Woman of
Beautiful Love

Early church fathers taught that as Christ is the new Adam, Mary is the new Eve. Down though the centuries, the Church has encouraged women to imitate the Mother of Jesus. While affirming the glories of Mary, at the same time the hierarchy and some theologians showed little regard for other women. A look at the writings of the great saints of the Church such as St. Augustine, St. Albert the Great, and St. Thomas Aquinas, among others reveals that woman has been regularly regarded as inferior to man.

The Scripture tells us that God created man and woman in His image. For centuries, however, theologians debated whether or not a woman was made in the image of God. They even taught that the Lord infused the soul into the male fetus much sooner than He did the female. Although the Holy Scripture tells us that God made woman to be a helper to man, St. Augustine, in a classic derogatory discourse regarding women, finds this difficult to understand, writing: "I don't see what sort of help she was created to provide man with, if one excludes the purpose of procreation. If woman is not given to man for help in bearing children, for what help could she be? To till the earth together? If help were needed for that, man would have been a better help for man. The same goes for comfort in solitude. How much more pleasure is it for life and conversation when two friends live together than when a man and a woman cohabitate." (*De genesi ad litteram* 9, 5–9).

Because of anti-feminist attitudes in theology down through the centuries, and which continue in some places until now, many women today are confused about their femininity. In their search for equality with men and freedom, many have lost their true feminine identity. They have attempted to be like men and have failed to achieve their true potential as women and have become "misbegotten men" as St. Albert the Great, the "Doctor Universalis" described women.

> "Woman is less qualified [than man] for moral behavior. Woman knows nothing of fidelity. Woman is a misbegotten man and has a faulty and defec-

tive nature. And, to put it briefly, one must be on one's guard with every woman, as if she were a poisonous snake and the horned devil. Her feelings drive woman toward every evil; just as reason impels man toward all good." (*Quaestiones super de animalibus* XV q. 11)

This brings to mind what one priest who received his seminary education in the United once told us. He said that in the seminary he was warned to be on guard against women, because every woman is a womb waiting to be fecundated.

Reeling from centuries of anti-feminine pessimism in the Church, many women have become rebellious and have tried to find themselves by self-assertion and denial of what they view as a patriarchal Church that attempts to keep them repressed. Although it does not exculpate him in any way, St. Albert was merely continuing a line of thought that was expressed by Aristotle who described women as inferior to men in virtue. The Greek philosopher described woman as a mutilated male, an imperfect creature ("On the Generation of Animals" 2, 3).

Such sexual pessimism was continued by St. Thomas Aquinas who, following his teacher St. Albert, also saw women as inferior, having less mental strength than men (II/II q. 49 a. 4). To Thomas, a female child resulted when something in the gestation period went awry and produced a female, because nature always intended to create a male.

At the same time that the male dominated Church honored Mary as the Immaculate Virgin and Mother undefiled because of her Immaculate Conception, all other women by comparison were naturally regarded as defiled. They seemed to forget that women are all immaculately conceived in the waters of the baptismal font through the regenerating power of Baptism, just as men are. Furthermore, the Mother of Jesus was so idealized that it became almost impossible for some woman to imitate her, especially for women of the twentieth century. She was a Queen—the woman on the pedestal in the church who was not related to their lives. She was a statue of marble that did not seem to have life. Many have complained they find it difficult to imitate a young maiden who lived in Nazareth two thousand years ago and had a marriage that does not resemble theirs.

Since Mary is the Mother of Jesus, women have been encouraged to imitate her maternity. It is easy for young mothers of small children to relate to Mary with the baby Jesus in her arms. However, in some periods of Church history, until quite recently, primarily male churchmen have seen woman as a baby factory that is to serve the man silently in the home without complaint.

In former ages, when the life span of woman was much shorter than it is today, most women probably died before their child bearing years came to a conclusion. Furthermore, since so many children died in infancy, it was necessary to have many babies in order to have adult male children to survive the death of their parents and inherit the family property and carry on the family name. Today relatively few children succumb to childhood diseases and women are living far beyond the cessation of their fertility. Often their grandchildren live in distant cities or states. The typical mother paradigm that many women lived in this country when their children were young no longer works for her.

How can the woman of today find her true femininity? How does a twenty-first century woman relate to Christ, Mary, and the Church?

Fortunately, John Paul II, following the example of Jesus, has a high regard for women and their friendship. Ever since his days as a student and later as a university professor in Poland, John Paul II has had a genuine liking and admiration for women. His teachings on the theology of the body will revolutionize the Church's attitudes toward women, once they have filtered down throughout academic circles in the Church and have penetrated the minds of the clergy, and finally have reached the entire Church.

In order to provide a total vision of man, or adequate anthropology, John Paul II presented his views on the theology of the body in a series of 129 talks given at his Wednesday audiences, beginning in September of 1979 and ending November 1984. On February 20, 1980 he posited: "The body and it alone is capable of making visible what is invisible, the spiritual and divine. It was created to transfer into the visible reality of the world the invisible mystery in God from time immemorial, and thus to be a sign of it." To make His mystery visible to us, God created man, as male and female, in His own image, so that this image would reflect the communion of the Persons of the Trinity. The relationship between man and woman is to be one of self-giving on the part of each of them. The pope explains:

> Genesis 2: 23–25 enables us to deduce that woman, who in the mystery of creation "is given" to man by the Creator, is "received," thanks to original innocence. That is, man as a gift accepts her. The Bible text is quite clear and limpid at this point. At the same time, the acceptance of the woman by the man and the very way of accepting her, become, as it were a first donation. In giving herself (from the very first moment in which, the mystery of creation, she was "given" to the man by the Creator) the woman "rediscovers herself" at the same time. This is because she has been accepted and welcomed, and because of the way in which she has been received by the man.

> So she finds herself again in the very fact of giving herself through a sincere gift of herself (cf GS 24), when she is accepted in the way in which the Creator wishes her to be, that is, "for her own sake," through her humanity and femininity. When the whole dignity of the gift is ensured in this acceptance,

through the offer of what she is in the whole truth of humanity and in the whole reality of her body and sex, of her femininity, she reaches the inner depth of her person and full possession of herself." (Wednesday audience Feb 6, 1980)

Similarly when the man accepts the gift of woman, she in turn receives him as gift. "Accepted in this way, he is enriched through this acceptance and welcoming of the gift of his own masculinity. Subsequently, this acceptance, in which the man finds himself again through the sincere gift of himself, becomes in him the source of a new and deeper enrichment of the women." Since the exchange is mutual, both find themselves again, are enriched and grow. In this way the human person becomes a gift in the freedom of love. The Pope explains in the audience of January 16, 1980: "Man or woman, in the context of their beatifying beginning, are free with the freedom of the gift. To remain in the relationship of the 'sincere gift of themselves' and to become such a gift for each other, through the whole of their humanity made of femininity and masculinity also in relation to that perspective which Genesis 2: 24 speaks of, they must be free precisely in this way."

In speaking of freedom, the pontiff equates it with mastery of oneself or self-control. By accepting each other the man and the woman affirm each other as persons and they create by their reciprocity a communion of persons and thus are made in the image of God, for God is a community of persons. Man—male and female—become the image of God not only by our humanity but also by our community of persons.

From this starting point John Paul II goes on the write more on Christian marriage, than any other pope before him ever has. But he does not stop with this, for his aim is to create a total vision, or complete anthropology. Applying his ideas on masculinity and femininity to the kingdom of God and those who renounce marriage for it, he sates: "If a man or a woman is capable of making a gift of himself for the kingdom of heaven, this proves in turn (and perhaps even more) that there is the freedom of the gift in the human body. It means that his body possesses a full nuptial meaning" (Wednesday January 16, 1980). Here John Paul II is referring to the eschatological wedding feast of Christ and His Bride the Church that will one day be celebrated.

As we know from the Genesis accounts Adam and Eve lost their innocence and the Second Person of the Trinity became man to save us from the state of sin into which our first parents plunged us with their disobedience. As He was dying on the cross and blood and water, symbolizing Eucharist and Baptism, poured from His wounded side, the Church, destined to be His bride, was born. This is in parallel to the Genesis account in which God formed Eve from a rib taken from Adam's side.

Mary, the Mother of Jesus, present on Calvary and given to St. John the Evangelist as mother, is the prototype of the Church. This teaching reminds us of the teaching of St. Ambrose that Mary is a type of the Church because in the mystery of the Church, which is both Virgin and Mother, Mary stands out as the great exemplar of both virginity and motherhood. The glorious Mother of our Redeemer is also the beloved daughter of the Eternal Father and temple of the Holy Spirit. As the documents of Vatican II state:

> She is clearly the mother of the members of Christ…since she has by her charity joined in bringing about the birth of believers, in the Church, who are members of its head, and as its type an outstanding model in faith and charity. The Catholic Church, taught by the Holy Spirit, honors her with filial affection and devotion as a most beloved mother. (414)

Assumed into heaven and intimately united to the Church, she continues to intercede for the brothers and sisters of Christ. As Mary is the prototype of the Church, the Church is also virgin and mother. As the documents of Vatican II explain, she is mother because she brings forth her children who are conceived by the Holy Spirit in the waters of baptism. She is a virgin because she "keeps in its entirety the faith she pledged to her spouse. Imitating the Mother of her Lord, and by the power of the Holy Spirit, she keeps intact faith, firm hope and sincere charity" (Vol I 420).

Because Mary is without spot or wrinkle, the Church contains that perfection to which Mary has already attained. The members of the Church striving for holiness turn to Mary, as the example of all virtues, by meditating on her life in the Word of God. "Seeking after the glory of Christ, the Church becomes more like her lofty type, and continually progresses in faith, hope, and charity, seeking and doing the will of God in all things." The documents of Vatican II rightly declare that she is the model of maternal love for all who take part in the Church's apostolic mission for the redemption of mankind (421). Furthermore, the documents look forward to the eschatological development of the church. "In the meantime, the Mother of Jesus in the glory which she possesses in body and soul in heaven is the image and beginning of the Church as it is to be perfected in the world to come" (422).

As the Church looks forward to the life of the world to come, John Paul II in his total vision of man looks forward also to it in his theology of the body. Interestingly, just when the pontiff was ready to present his thought on the resurrection of the body, he was shot by Mehmet Ali Agca on May 13, 1981 and was unable to continue with his ideas and audiences until November 11, 1981. No doubt during his fight for life over death as he lay hospitalized, he had ample opportunity to consider his brush with death and the hope of the resurrection.

John Paul II began his discussion on the eschatological dimensions of his theology of the body by speaking of the Scripture in which the Sadducees question Christ on marriage and heaven by asking about whose wife a certain hypothetical woman would be in heaven, having married seven men in this life. Since we know that the Sadducees did not believe in the resurrection of the body as the Pharisees did, we understand that they were merely baiting Christ. The Lord explains that in heaven there will be no marriage; all will be virgins. The resurrection will bring a new submission of the body to the spirit. The body will be spiritualized; our humanity will be assumed by the divinity of God. John Paul II explains:

> Participation in the divine nature, participation in the interior life of God Himself, permeation of what is essentially human by what is essentially divine, will then reach its peak so that the life of the human spirit will arrive at such fullness which previously had been absolutely inaccessible to it. (Nov 11, 1981)

Completely immersed in the vision of God, man and woman will experience truth and love in exceedingly great abundance such has never before been possible for them. What the pope has referred to as the "nuptial meaning of the body," ever since the first audiences of September 1979, is fully attained and realized.

Commenting on the nuptial meaning of the body, Father Richard Hogan explains: "The human body reveals to human persons through its nuptial meaning that we are called to love, to give ourselves in imitation of the Trinity. The nuptial meaning of the body is the understanding in each of our intellects that we are created to give ourselves to one another in a God-like self-giving, life-affirming and life-giving love" (Hogan "Intro").

The pope concludes by observing that in heaven in the beatific vision we will be linked to all others and especially united to those we knew here in this life. He also observes that there are those in this life who want to bypass the nuptial life in this world and pursue the spiritual donation of themselves to Christ in anticipation of the great nuptial feast of heaven. John Paul makes it crystal clear that the fact that God created us male and female is at the very basis of his total vision, or anthropology. We are male or female and will be for all eternity.

Throughout the history of the Church many of the saints have found their masculine or feminine counterpart and have risen to greater heights of holiness, because they did. We recall how St. Margaret Mary Alacoque drew a picture of the Sacred Heart, a large heart, for St. Claude de la Columbière and then drew their two small hearts together inside of it. They helped each other become saints, as did St. Francis and St. Clare, and St Jeanne de Chantal and St. Francis de Sales. It is told that when Jeanne de Chantal viewed the deceased body of her spiritual father in his coffin and bent to give him a last embrace, his hand patted her on the head as a witness of their love for one another. St. Jerome depended on St. Paula for consolation as they lived in Bethlehem while he was translating the Vulgate. He complained bitterly when she died that God had taken his angel away from him to sing in heavenly choirs. When one thinks of St. Vincent de Paul, one automatically remembers St. Louise de Marillac and how together they founded the Sisters of Charity. More recently, Pius XII, that ascetical and unworldly seeming pope, had a long abiding friendship that lasted until his death with Mother Pascalina Lehnert, a woman who was known in the Vatican as La Popessa.

Earlier in this chapter we raised the question as to how women are to relate to Mary and the Church. We will now attempt to answer that question in light of the theology of the body that upholds the beauty of femininity in this world and in the world to come. How can women find Mary and become like her? Certainly not by gazing at cold plaster statues. She is a vibrant woman who is very closely united to the Church. You will find her in Holy Scripture in the scenes of the nativity, at the wedding in Cana, on Calvary when blood and water flowed from the side of Christ. You will find her at Pentecost in the upper room when the Holy Spirit was poured out on the nascent Church.

You will find her in the Church for she inhabits the Church and it is her holiness that makes the Church a Bride that is without spot or wrinkle. She is represented in all the spiritual and corporeal works of mercy of the Church.

You will find her at the baptismal font as her children are born of water and the Spirit. She whispers "amen" when you say your penance after reconciliation. You will find her with Holy Mother Church, nourishing her children and leading them to Jesus. Look for her most especially at the liturgy of the Eucharist, for it is the representation in an unbloody manner of Christ's death, passion, and resurrection. At mass we are present on Calvary 2000 years ago and Mary is standing with us, offering her son to the Father together with us. Since Mary is the prototype of the Church, cannot the Church also be said to be a reflection or type of the Virgin Mother? The beauty we see in the Church is a reflection of the beauty of the Mother of Jesus, the Mother of Beautiful Love.

As we come to understand what John Paul II is saying about the theology of the body, we realize that women are to identify themselves with the Church and with Mary. There they see their femininity most clearly and become what God intends them to be. While men by their masculinity identify with Jesus, women identify in their femininity with Mary and the Church. As Jesus is the new Adam, Mary is the New Eve. However, we must remember that we are dealing with symbolism. When we use symbolism, we do so to express some basic truths. However, the symbolism is not the truths themselves, but a way of presenting the truths. For this reason, symbolism is not always consistent. It can only take us so far in finding truth. We know that Mary is the Mother of Jesus, but that she is also the New Eve, the prototype of the Church and, as such, she is part of the Bride of Christ. We behold her in Bethlehem kissing His baby feet and hands worshipfully in adoration. We see her assumed into heaven where she dwells in the heart of the Trinity and we know that because she is there, we too will be taken up into heaven and live in the heart of God for all eternity.

Picture the Trinity as a great triangle with each angle representing one of the persons of God. Picture Mary and the Church as a circle enclosed inside the triangle. Love flows out from each of the persons of the Trinity in our diagram going through the inside of the triangle to each of the other persons of the Trinity, with the love converging in the center circle, the glorified Church, containing the Mother of God.

Symbolism is meant to convey truth, not to be consistent. We learn from John Paul II's teaching on the theology of the body that sexual differences are important and eternal. Women cannot be men, nor men, women. Each has his place in God's nuptial plan for our glorification. Men are also members of the Church, representing the male Christ The symbolism is overlapping here for all the people of God are members of Mother Church.

We in the Church need to do more to affirm woman's role and dignity in the kingdom. Women need to enter more deeply into the mysteries of Mary and the glories of the Church, working as teachers, authors, theologians, nurses, doctors, doing all the spiritual and corporal works of mercy, knowing that in so doing they are becoming like Mary and more closely united to the Church and Christ. By affirming woman's role and dignity in the kingdom, she will freely be able to make her self-donation to Christ and His Church. She will become the woman of beautiful love.

The theology of the body teaches us that women cannot be priests—they cannot be male or play a male role. In trying to become like men they lose their identity and become merely caricatures of the women they are meant to be.

When women strive to become like the Virgin Mother of Jesus and Virgin Mother Church, the Church needs to affirm them, receive them and accept them so that they may grow in self-realization of who they are to be in God—virgin, bride, and mother—companions—the women of beautiful love.

Live Free in the Spirit!

We cannot become the people God wants us to be without the gifts and the charisms of the Holy Spirit. We who have been baptized and confirmed have received the Holy Spirit, but perhaps He is dormant in our souls. We once heard someone say you can pour chocolate syrup into a glass of milk and the syrup will go to the bottom of the glass. In order to get the benefit of the chocolate, you have to stir it up. This recalls what St. Paul wrote to Timothy on whom he had laid hands to ordain him. "I admonish you, that you stir up the grace of God which is in you, by the imposition of my hands. For God has not given us the spirit of fear but of power, and of love, and of sobriety" (2 Ti 1: 5–7). So we too must stir up the grace of God that we have received. We must strive to guard and nourish the living flame of love that has been set burning in our hearts and which the world and all the forces of evil try to extinguish. God has given us the Holy Spirit who is an invincible power against all the evil forces that can ever attack us. The Spirit gives us His gifts to assure our victory over sin—the world, the flesh, and all evil powers.

Listed by Isaiah in ascending order, the gifts of the Holy Spirit are these: fear, piety, knowledge, fortitude, counsel, understanding, and wisdom (11: 2). The gift of fear keeps us from offending God, because He is all good and deserving of all our love. This is not a servile fear, by which we cringe before the Omnipotent God, but a filial fear, a fear like that of a child not wanting to offend a well-beloved parent. As his sons and daughters, we stand before the majesty of the Most High in awe, thankful that the gift of holy fear causes us to flee the slightest sin and everything that would separate us from Him. Corresponding to the beatitude of the poor in spirit, it even helps us to be temperate and chaste. When the Holy Spirit touches the soul and infuses it with holy fear, we become afraid of offending God.

The gift of piety fills our hearts with a filial love for our Heavenly Father, giving us fervor for the things of God and His service. Helping us to glorify God with loving hearts, it completes the virtue of religion and corresponds to the beatitude blessed are the meek, making it possible for God's children to live the beatitude. It makes us recognize that everything is in God's loving hands and that everything that happens is for the good for those that love the Lord and are called according to his purpose. We rejoice when good things happen and praise God when things seem to go awry, knowing that everything is in His hands and He loves us more than we can ever fathom.

The gift of knowledge makes it possible for us to see things from God's point of view, impressing upon us that the things of God are eternal, by revealing to us that the world with all its honors is fleeting and transitory. As the book of Ecclesiastes teaches: "Vanity of vanities; all is vanity save to fear God and keep His commandments. All things are hard: man cannot explain them by word. The eye is not filled with seeing, neither is the ear filled with hearing" (Ec 1: 8). When we perceive the vanity of earthly things as we read about them in Ecclesiastes, we become submissive to the inspirations of the Spirit of God and come to hate evil, turn away from it, and love what is good, and embrace it. This gift makes it possible for us to live the beatitude blessed are they who mourn.

The gift of fortitude completes the virtue of fortitude and corresponds to the beatitude of those who hunger and thirst after justice. It gives us patience to endure and suffer more than would be humanly possible without God's grace. It can make us truly heroic like John of Arc, burning at the stake, while crying out the name of Jesus.

The gift of counsel corresponds to the virtue of prudence, making it possible for us to know what to do in difficult situations. How many times have we tried to find solutions to problems and could not, until the Holy Spirit gave us penetrating insights of counsel that enabled us to find the right answer. The gift of counsel is very helpful in finding our vocation in life and solving moral problems. It corresponds to the beatitude blessed are the merciful and makes it possible for the Christian to live that beatitude.

The gift of understanding is a wonderfully helpful gift. The gift of understanding helps us to probe the mysteries of faith and reveals things to us that we could never discover on our own. It enlightens us when we read the Word of God, hear a sermon, or when we do our spiritual reading, making it possible for us to enter into the mysteries of grace. It corresponds to the beatitude blessed are the pure in heart for they shall see God. The gift of understanding lets us see God, as in a glass darkly, when we read Holy Scripture, pray, and receive the sacraments, especially the Eucharist. This is a great gift and one we should beseech the Holy Spirit to give us in abundance.

The gifts are listed here in ascending order, from the lowest to the highest. The gift of wisdom, corresponding to the virtue of charity, is the greatest of the gifts just as charity is the greatest of the virtues. It makes us relish the things of

God and increases our love for Him by making it possible for us to taste and see that the Lord is good. Wisdom will guide us to holiness and righteousness, lead us to embracing God's Holy Will, and to accepting joyfully His Loving Providence. It helps us to see things from His perspective and fills us with His peace. Corresponding to the beatitude blessed are the peacemakers, this gift makes it possible for us to live this beatitude. Our God of peace calls peacemakers his children.

We need to beseech the Holy Spirit to infuse us with all his gifts in abundance so that we may securely walk through the snares of this life and eventually come to Him in glory. He is always present in the souls of the just—those who are in a state of grace. When we listen for His inspirations and then when He gives them, and when we try to do what He wants us to do, He lavishly pours His gifts into our souls. Let us always be docile in His hands and He will fill our souls with joy. As we grow in grace, the Holy Spirit infuses us increasingly with faith, hope, and love and fills us with His gifts making it possible for us to live the beatitudes and travel on the straight road to heaven.

Let us open our hearts to receive the Holy Spirit; He will give us power, love, and self-control making it possible for us to live the Gospel of Christ, which no one can do without His help. He will supply all our needs; heal our bodies, restore our families, and free us of addictions. With God all things are possible; without Him we can do nothing.

When the Spirit fell and infused the Church on the day of Pentecost as the Apostles and the Mother of Jesus waited in the Upper Room, the Spirit made Himself manifest gloriously through the charisms that the people received. By charisms we mean special gifts that make it possible for a Christian to perform a special service for the Church.

In 1 Corinthians, St. Paul gives a detailed accounting of the charisms of the early Church. The people on Pentecost were so overwhelmed by the tremendous outpouring of the Holy Spirit and the grace of God that some people thought they were drunk on new wine. Men who had been cowards on Good Friday became strong and heroic. St. Peter boldly preached the Gospel of Christ with bravery and valor such as he had never known before.

The most commonly received charism was the speaking in tongues. People were able to speak and understand languages that they had never before used. Some people interpreted the unknown tongues that some of them spoke. Still others prophesied. Everyone received a manifestation of the Holy Spirit. Because of these manifestations, many people came to believe in the Holy Spirit and the Gospel of Christ.

At Pentecost, some people received the charism that made it possible for them to discern spirits. Other people received the charisms of healing, miracles, or speaking words of wisdom and knowledge.

When some began to complain that they had not received the charism someone else had, St. Paul tried to explain to them that the main thing was that they had all received the same Spirit. He further explained that the greatest gift was the ability to prophesy and that they should strive to prophesy. He explicitly told them that the charisms are for the building up of the Church.

Christ is the same yesterday, today, and forever and so likewise is the Holy Spirit. The charisms He lavished on the people in the New Testament times, He will give to us, if we ask Him for them. He will move in us and we will experience His presence as He manifests Himself and He will testify to us of the marvelous revelation of Jesus Christ and His grace within us. We need His charisms, for without the Holy Spirit we cannot even confess that Jesus is Lord, as St. Paul explains. "And no man can say the Lord Jesus, but by the Holy Ghost" (1 Cor 12: 3).

The word charism means spiritual gift and it indicates redemption by God's grace. A person who possesses charisms is a charismatic. The charisms are gifts that God gives to enable people to do specific ministries in the Church. They especially give joy to those who receive them. Often they are the source of healing, wisdom, and even miracles and bring peace to the believer who receives them.

Glossolalia, or the speaking in tongues, was very prevalent in the early Church and St. Paul said he spoke in tongues very much. Today people in the Charismatic Renewal are encouraged to speak in tongues and are edified by the practice. We too can receive the gift of speaking in tongues, if we do not stifle it, when it begins to rise up in us. It can be alarming to feel strange words forming within and trying to find utterance. There is nothing to fear. We just let the words flow from us. The Scripture teaches that we do not know how we should pray, but that the Holy Spirit will pray within us. "Likewise the Spirit also helps our infirmity. For we know not what we should pray for, as we ought, but the Spirit Himself asks for us with unspeakable groanings. And He that searches the hearts, knows what the Spirit desires, because He asks for the saints according to God" (Rom 9: 26–27). The Holy Spirit teaches us how to pray according to God's will and although the sounds of an unknown tongue coming from us may baffle us, the Heavenly Father understands them.

Speaking in tongues serves for the building up of the Church. There should always be an interpretation for any glossolalia that occurs during a prayer meeting.

The charism of wisdom as discussed by St. Paul is really the same as the gift of wisdom listed by Isaiah. The purpose of the wisdom that the Holy Spirit grants is to glorify the Christian. This wisdom is especially helpful in figuring out how to solve the problems that we encounter every day. In giving us His wisdom, the Holy Spirit intends to sanctify us and help us on our way to eternal life and glory and to fill us with His joy that never ends.

Whenever we are beset by a problem, we should ask the Holy Spirit for His guidance and direction. Sometimes others might receive a "word of wisdom" for us to help us live better lives. Resembling prophecy, a "word of wisdom" can often help us tremendously to understand what God is doing with our lives. We know that He has a magnificent plan to give us happiness, joy, and peace so that our lives will reflect His goodness to all who know us.

We must always consciously try to conform to God's will for our lives and to do this we need the charism of wisdom to enable us to see our lives from God's point of view. Because wisdom is such a great charism we should constantly pray to receive it, remembering always to thank Him for this and all His other gifts. Wisdom is especially to be sought, for it unites our souls to God and draws Him near to us.

Often times one hears someone speak "a word of knowledge." This charism is especially helpful in daily life. It helps the mother to know what her child is doing and if there is anything wrong with him. It resembles intuition, but it is really a charism that the Holy Spirit gives to us to help us live our lives most fully.

The gift of miracles is another of the Holy Spirit's wonderful charisms. In the case of a miracle, God suspends or breaks the natural laws and definitely demonstrates His power. There are many miracles in the Holy Scripture, but they still occur today and not just at Lourdes or Fatima. Wherever the power of God is, miracles can happen. Everything is possible with God and we should always keep our minds and hearts open for the miraculous to occur. God can work a miracle anywhere at anytime, whenever He pleases, in anyway He wishes. In the Holy Scripture, we see Jesus healing the sick everywhere He goes. He is the same Lord today that He was in Galilee and Judea. Expect Him to give you your miracle, for He tells us He will give us anything we ask of Him if we have faith. Our Jesus is a healing Lord and we should take all our illnesses to Him to be cured. He heals in the Eucharist and also when a person of faith lays hands upon an ailing person and prays for healing. We accept and receive our healing as soon as we request it of Him. The greatest healing of all will be the resurrection of our bodies when they rise in newness of life, glorified, never more to die.

Perhaps the charism we might receive is what St. Paul calls the charism of helps. Some people feel called on in a special way to help others. There are lots of opportunities for service in the parishes today. If we feel led to help others, we can serve by driving older people to the doctor or the grocery store, by babysitting, by visiting the sick or in a myriad of different ways. There are countless ways we can help others.

The Holy Spirit may give us a charism for teaching catechism to children. There is a great need for that in the Church today, because catechesis has been neglected for a long time and many young people know practically nothing about their faith. Sadly, in recent times those who try to mix New Age and their own opinions taken from other Christian denominations together with Catholic doctrine have taught some incorrectly.

As St. Paul wrote, prophecy is the greatest of the charisms and one we might hope to obtain. To prophesy does not mean to foretell the future. Rather it means to speak publicly for God by proclaiming His will. To speak for God in prophecy, we must be certain that God supports what we are saying. The prophet both edifies and consoles the persons to whom his prophecy is addressed as He invites them to conform to the Holy Will of God.

Before we begin to prophesy, we must be sure we ourselves are in the will of God. The charism of prophecy is especially invaluable for a priest who is trying to help his flock find God. Before we prophesy, we need to sit at the feet of Jesus and listen attentively to what He will say to us. A good place to do is this is before the reserved Eucharist in our churches. If what we prophesy is true, it will bring peace to our souls. If it does not bring peace, we will know that we have not prophesied rightly and we will have to try harder to discern the spirits that move us.

By the discernment of spirits, we can determine if the person who prophesies is speaking for God, for himself, for an angelic spirit—a good angel or an evil one. If a prophecy does not agree with the Word of God, it is a false prophecy. It must also conform to the teachings of the Church to be considered true and it should accord with the faith of the people in the pews.

We need to pray to receive the charisms of the Holy Spirit, avoiding doing anything that would stifle them, and when we receive them, we should cherish them and thank God for them.

"Holy Spirit we welcome you into our minds, hearts, and souls. We welcome your gifts and charisms, accepting them as proofs of Your love for us. May we always listen for your inspirations and when we receive them, may we always hasten to do what You want of us. Help us to overcome our weaknesses and teach us righteousness. Lead us in the paths of Your salvation and protect us from all evil. Guide us in living victorious and resplendent lives in Christ. In Jesus name we pray. Amen."

Live Free from Sickness and Disease

The gospel writers present Jesus as a healer. Matthew tells us that He went around in all Galilee, teaching in the synagogues, and preaching the gospel of the kingdom, healing every kind of sickness and infirmity, with His fame extending even throughout Syria (Mt 4: 23–24). One particular cure is described as taking place when Jesus, followed by a great multitude, comes down from the mountain where he preached the sermon on the beatitudes. Something very unusual happens. A leper, Luke describes him as "a man full of leprosy" (Lk 3: 12), suddenly appears and "falling on his face" before Jesus humbles himself in a way one would not expect of a Jew (Luke 5: 12).

How alarmed the multitude must be! In order to comprehend the full significance of this event, we need to understand the plight of the leper in Jewish society that regarded leprosy as a scourge of God. In the Old Testament, leprosy was inflicted on Moses' sister Miriam as a judgment, because she opposed his marriage to the Ethiopian woman that he probably married after the death of Zipporah, the Midionite. Similarly Gehazi, Elisha's servant was struck by leprosy, because he fraudulently obtained money and clothing from Naaman after Elisha cleansed him of his leprosy. King Uzziah was smitten with leprosy because he invaded the realm of the priests in the temple and offered incense.

The Law of Moses imputed pollution to anyone who contracted leprosy so that the leper was ostracized from the community. Rabbis would throw stones at lepers who tried to approach them so that they were cut off spiritually as well as physically from all contact with society. However, there was in the synagogue a small separate room, ten feet high and six feet wide, called the Mechitsah, set aside for them. At times lepers, for companionship, would live in groups outside the towns. To announce their condition, they had to go about with their garments rent and their cloaks covering their mouths, as they cried, "Unclean, unclean." Not allowed the freedom of the walled towns like Jerusalem, all were generally treated as dead men.

It was unlawful to greet a leper or get closer to one than four cubits or six feet. On a windy day, a leper had to keep a distance of one hundred cubits up wind from everyone. No doubt the physical repulsion of the leper's sores and his stench were enough to keep people at quite a distance from him.

With crusting sores and inflammation, the disease makes its first appearances on the skin, but it gradually proceeds to eat away fingers and toes. Gradually rotting the leper as he lives, the disease proceeds even to the marrow of the bones, making his life a living death. Because leprosy was generally believed to be an outward sign of inner spiritual corruption, people had little sympathy or compassion for lepers.

Even in quite recent times, people believed leprosy to be transmitted by sexually immoral people and the result of syphilis. Fr. Albert Montiton, a Frenchman that was sent to help Father Damien of Molokai, aka Blessed Joseph de Veuster (1840–1889), accused him of sexual immorality, because he had contracted leprosy by taking care of lepers. In 1883, after twenty-two years on Molokai, Father Damien had lost the feeling in his one leg and his foot was reddened. Two years later a leprous sore appeared on his ear lobe and his eyebrows fell off.

There was still much ignorance about leprosy in the late nineteenth century. It is now known that leprosy is an infectious disease caused by the mycobacterium leprae, or Hansen's bacillus, named after Dr. Gerhard Hansen (1841–1912) who first observed it. Damien caught it simply by taking care of the people in his community.

The disease is prevalent in many parts of the world and continues to be a social problem in countries like Paraguay where lepers are still regarded as outcasts and for this reason refuse to report their disease and seek treatment for it, although there are a number of drugs today that successfully treat it. The Society of Lepers in Paraguay, Patronato de Leprosos del Paraguay, estimates that there are approximately twelve hundred lepers there.

Considering the impact of a leper venturing into society, no doubt the multitude following Jesus was astonished to see a leper approach Him. They probably were waiting to see if Jesus would stone the man and drive him away as other rabbis did. Obviously, the leper had heard a lot about Jesus and had perhaps watched from a distance and saw His compassion in dealing with the afflicted. With utter confidence he draws near to Jesus, falls with his face on the ground and totally submits to Him.

Although there was no prescribed rabbinic remedy for leprosy, this leper was absolutely confident that Jesus could heal him, or cleanse him, as people said when speaking of leprosy. Humbly, the leper says to Jesus simply, "Lord, if you will, you can make me clean" (Mt 8: 2).

No doubt the onlookers gasped as they watched Jesus. They knew that He had to avoid contact with the leper and that He would be unclean if he allowed the man to get nearer to him than four cubits or six feet. They believed that Jesus would risk a horrible infection, if He touched the leper. Compassionately and without hesitation, "Jesus stretching forth his hand, touches Him, saying: "I will, be made clean." Immediately his leprosy is cleansed (Mt. 8: 3). Jesus then directs him to go to the priests as the Mosaic Law commands and receive certification that he no longer has leprosy. Luke tells us that after this miracle "the fame of Him went abroad the more, and great multitudes came together to hear, and to be healed by Him of their infirmities" (Lk 5: 15).

We learn, from the story of this leper, a great deal about divine healing. If we want to be healed, we should approach Jesus like the leper did, bowing before Him and adoring Him with absolute confidence that He is able to heal us. Very humbly we pray, like the leper, "Lord, if you will, you can heal me." And in faith we know that He will do so.

When Jesus preaches with power and authority in the synagogue of Capernaum on the Sabbath, near the beginning of His public ministry, there is a man present with an unclean spirit or in Luke's words "an unclean devil" (Mk 1: 23, Lk 4: 33). Although the gospel writers do not give the details, we can picture the demoniac as interrupting Jesus' teaching by crying out: "What have we to do with you, Jesus of Nazareth? Are you come to destroy us? I know who you are, the Holy One of God" (Mk 1: 24). Speaking not to the man himself, but directly to the demon, Jesus silences him immediately with these words: "Speak no more, and go out of the man" (Mk 1: 25). Apparently, the man convulsed and was thrown down in the midst of the people. The gospel, according to Luke, reports: "And when the devil had thrown him into the midst, he went out of him, and hurt him not at all" (4: 35). Mark gives us this additional information: "And the unclean spirit tearing him, and crying out with a loud voice, went out of him (1: 26).

Overwhelmed by witnessing the power of Jesus in casting out the demon from the man, the people who are there become very much afraid. "And they were all amazed, insomuch that they questioned among themselves, saying: What thing is this? What is this new doctrine? For with power He commands even the unclean spirits, and they obey him" (Mk 1: 27). Notice that the dramatic cleansing of the demoniac highlights Jesus' teaching and makes people curious about His doctrine. The episode causes such a commotion that people quickly hear about it in all parts of Galilee. Luke records that "the fame of Him was published into every place in the country" (Lk 4: 37).

Immediately upon leaving the synagogue, Jesus, together with James and John, goes to the house of Simon and Andrew on the shores of the Sea of Galilee. Learning that Simon's mother-in-law is in bed with a high fever, Jesus goes to her. Standing over her, He commands the fever to leave. Taking her by the hand, He lifts her up and the fever is instantly gone. To show how complete the healing is, both Mark and Luke report that the woman immediately begins ministering to their needs (Mk 1: 31, Lk 4: 39).

With the news of the healing of Simon's mother-in-law spreading fast throughout the area, many, many people who are sick or possessed by demons are brought to Jesus that very evening. Apparently the whole town turns out. Jesus lays His hands on every one of them and heals them all. Devils leave many of them crying out: "You are the Son of God." Silencing them, Jesus rebukes them and will not let them speak (Lk 2: 40–41). One does not entertain the conversation of demons even though they speak the truth.

Interestingly, the demons recognize Jesus while the Scribes and Pharisees for the most part fail to do so. They are fully aware of the punishment that they will receive, when they are finally thrust into the abyss. The demons that Jesus casts into the swine in the country of the Gerasens also recognize and cry out in a similar fashion: "What have we to do with you, Jesus Son of God? Are you come here to torment us before the time?" (Mt 8: 28). They are referring to their future punishment when they will be cast down into hell. As James says in his epistle—the devils believe and tremble (Jas 2: 19). It is only human beings who deny the existence of hell. The demonic forces know that Christ is Lord and that they have to submit to Him and that their doom is sealed. It is as St. Paul states:

> He humbled himself, becoming obedient unto death, even to the death of the cross. For which cause God also has exalted him, and has given Him a name which is above all names, that in the name of Jesus every knee should bow, of those that are in heaven, on earth, and under the earth, and that every tongue should confess that the Lord Jesus Christ is in the glory of God the Father. (Php 2: 8)

Another remarkable healing is that of the slave of the Roman centurion. Matthew describes this healing in detail as taking place in Capernaum when a certain centurion, a Roman soldier and the commander of one hundred men, comes to Jesus requesting that he heal his slave who is tormented with palsy or paralysis. When Jesus agrees to go to the man's house and heal his servant, the Roman centurion very humbly states that he is not worthy of the honor of having Jesus come to his house, but he knows that Jesus can cure him simply by speaking the words. So great was the pagan centurion's faith that Jesus marvels at it, commenting that he has not seen such faith in Israel among God's chosen people. Immediately Jesus tells him that his servant is healed. "And Jesus said to the centurion: 'Go, and as you have believed, so be it done to you.' And the servant was healed at the same hour" (Mt 8: 13).

Just as the others that Jesus healed, the centurion has complete confidence in Jesus' power to heal. He has probably heard much of Jesus' reputation as a healer and humbly requests that He heal his slave. His great humility and utter confidence obtain the healing he desires. We should imitate his humility and faith, if we seek healing from the Lord.

Matthew relates Jesus' healing of human sickness and infirmity to the fulfillment of the prophecy of Isaiah that the Messiah bore our diseases and infirmities, the point being that because Jesus bore them, we do not have to.

> Surely he hath borne our infirmities and carried our sorrows: and we have thought him as it were a leper, and as one struck by God and afflicted. But he was wounded for our iniquities, he was bruised for our sins. The chastisement of our peace was upon him, and by his bruises we are healed. (Isaiah 53: 4–5)

Similarly the Apostle Peter speaks of the sufferings of Jesus being the cause of our healing. He writes, "Who His own self bore our sins in His body upon the tree, that we, being dead to sins, should live to justice, by whose stripes you were healed" (1 Pe 2: 24). Notice that he says we were healed by His stripes, the awful wounds on his back laid open by the barbed thongs that dug into His flesh. We *were* healed. Out healing has been accomplished and now all that remains is for us to claim it. Jesus will heal us just as readily as He healed the people of the first century, if we humbly ask Him to, believing in faith that He can and will do it.

Another case of healing in the gospels involves another man with palsy or paralysis. Because there was such a large crowd around Jesus in the house where He was ministering, the sick man's friends that had great faith opened up a hole in the roof and lowered the man together with his bed down into the house and lay him right at the feet of Jesus. Upon seeing their faith, Jesus says immediately "Man, your sins are forgiven you."

Upon hearing Jesus forgive the man his sins, the Scribes and the Pharisees become indignant and accuse Him in their minds of blasphemy, because only God can forgive sins. Knowing their thoughts, Jesus asks them "Which is easier to say—your sins are forgiven or to say arise and walk?" So that they would know that He has power to forgive sins, He speaks to the man sick with palsy. "I say to you, arise, take up your bed, and go into your house." Immediately the man who was paralyzed is cured, picks up his bed, and goes home, perfectly well with his sins forgiven (Lk 5: 18–26). Once again great faith leads to healing. The people who witnessed this healing were astonished, wondered and glorified God, saying: "We never saw the like!" (Mk 3: 12). Because of this and other healings, a great multitude followed Jesus to the seashore where He taught them.

The miraculous healings reinforce His teaching, and His teaching reinforces the miracles. We see some basic principles at work that will help us to live free from sickness and disease. The miracles attract people to listen to the Lord's teaching. Everywhere the gospel is preached such healings should occur. Miraculous cures are especially to be seen when the gospel is preached to people who have never heard it before, such as in pagan countries.

The miracles of Jesus cause great consternation among the Scribes and the Pharisees, the professionally religious people of Israel. They simply do not know what to make of Him. Consider what happens when Jesus goes to Naim with his disciples and a great multitude of followers. When he approaches the city's gate, a dead man is being carried out with his mother, a widow, and a large gathering of the citizens of the town in attendance. Because the mother is weeping bitter tears over the death of her only son, Jesus is moved with mercy and compassion. Telling her not to cry, he draws near and touches the coffin. Everything comes to a standstill with everyone watching to see what Jesus will do next. He speaks saying: "Young man, I say to you, arise." With amazement the people watch as the man that was dead sits up in his coffin and begins talking (Lk 7: 11–16). Events like this are more than the Scribes and Pharisees can endure.

Jesus' kind regard for women is shown in his healing of the woman who had been suffering from uterine bleeding for twelve years. Mark tells us that she had spent all her money on doctors and received no relief, but continued to get worse. In order to understand her situation, we have to consider how her fellow Jews regard her. Not only has she become weakened by the constant loss of blood, she is suffering from ritual uncleanness. According to Jewish law, a menstruating woman had to be separated from other people during the menses and for seven days afterwards—or about 2 weeks out of every four, almost half of the time. On the eight day after the bleeding ceased, she had to give the priest two turtledoves or young pigeons at the door of the tabernacle of the testimony. He offered one for sin and the other for holocaust and prayed for her before the Lord (Lev 15: 29).

Everyone that touched her during her period was automatically unclean until evening. Everything she slept on, or sat on during her menstrual period was automatically defiled. Anyone, who touched her bed or anything on which she sat, had to bathe and wash his clothes, but still remained unclean until evening. A man who had sex with a menstruating woman was unclean for seven days and every bed he slept on was considered defiled. Leviticus 15: 25 states that if a woman continues bleeding after her period should be over, she is unclean as long as the bleeding continues.

For twelve years this poor woman had to live separate from others. She was not even permitted to go to the temple or mingle with crowds in the streets. Not permitted to have sex with her husband, she could not have children.

Desperately the woman in the Scripture with the issue of blood slips through the crowd, probably hoping that no one would recognize her and cry "Unclean!" Approaching Jesus from the back, she hopes just to touch the hem of his robe to find healing, knowing full well that her touch would render Him ritually unclean. The tassels on garments had a special significance because the Lord had directed them to put them on their garments with a blue thread in them. These tassels were to serve as a reminder of the commandments of God as an aid in keeping the Law of Moses (Nu 15: 38–40). Regarding the practice of touching the tassels on Jesus' garments, Mark reports that, wherever Jesus went, people put their sick in the streets and begged Him that they might touch the hem of His garment and as many who touched Him in way were healed (Mk 6: 56).

Apparently greatly weakened by the continual loss of blood, the woman who has been suffering for twelve years timidly approaches Jesus hoping to be unperceived and bends over and touches the tassels of His robe. Instantaneously, the bleeding stops. Jesus perceives her touch and says, "Who touched me?" To which Peter replies that many people are pressing around Him and it is impossible to say.

"Somebody has touched me, for I perceive that virtue is gone out of me."

Mark tells us that He looked for the woman who had touched him. Obviously Jesus knew that it was a woman.

When the woman knows that she cannot keep hidden, she comes trembling before Jesus and falls down in front of him, confessing that she touched Him and was instantly healed. Reassuringly Jesus says: "Daughter, your faith has made you whole; go your way in peace" (Lk 8: 40–48).

No sooner is this woman healed, because of her faith, than someone else's pain and suffering is brought to Jesus' attention. A man named Jairus, a ruler of the synagogue, comes and falls at Jesus feet begging Him to come to his house to heal his eleven-year-old daughter who is dying. Compassionately Jesus says to him: "Fear not, believe only, and she shall be safe."

Together with Jairus and his wife and Peter, James, and John, Jesus goes to the house of the afflicted girl. As the parents mourn for the girl, Jesus says to them "Weep not; she is not dead, but is sleeping."

At this remark, Luke, the physician, reports, people who are gathered around scornfully laugh at Jesus, because they know she is dead. But Jesus takes the girl by the hand and simply says: "Maid, arise." Immediately she does and Jesus directs her parents to give her something to eat. Once more faith calls forth a miracle from Jesus (Lk 8: 55).

Luke also recounts how Jesus cleansed the devils from a man in the country of the Gerasens. Interestingly, when the devils leave the man and he is completely normal, the man wants to stay with Jesus, but Jesus tells him: "Return to your house, and tell what great things God has done to you." The man does as he is told and goes through the whole city telling the great things that have been done for him (Lk 8: 26–42). Similarly when we receive healing from Jesus, we must testify to the wonderful things He has done for us. We note that Jesus forgave the sins of the man suffering from palsy or paralysis before He healed him. If we are ill, we should confess our sins and try to live in the will of God.

The apostles also began healing when Jesus sent them out two by two, giving them power over unclean spirits (Mk 6: 7). He told them to preach saying: "The kingdom of heaven is at hand. Heal the sick, raise the dead, cleanse the lepers, and cast out devils; freely have you received, freely give (Mt 10: 8). Mark relates: "They cast out many devils, and anointed with oil many that were sick, and healed them" (Mk 6: 13).

Not only did Jesus give power to heal to the apostles, he gave it to all believers. Just before He ascended to His Father He spoke these words:

> "And these signs shall follow them that believe. In my name they shall cast out devils; they shall speak with new tongues. They shall take up serpents; and if they shall drink any deadly thing, it shall not hurt them; they shall lay their hands upon the sick, and they shall recover."

Mark concludes his gospel account by saying:

> And the Lord Jesus, after he had spoken to them, was taken up into heaven, and sits on the right hand of God. But they going forth preached everywhere, the Lord working withal, and confirming the word with signs that followed. (Mk 16: 17–20)

Jesus is Lord and the forces of darkness must always bow before Him in submission. He gives us advice about how to obtain grace and favor when we pray.
He tells us that we will receive answers to our prayers, if we believe that we will
(Mt 11: 24). If we ask, we will receive; if we seek we will find; and if we knock,
doors will open (Mt 7: 7). He assures us that everyone who asks, receives; all who
seek, find; and all who knock find an opening. Reminding us that no human
father will give his son a stone, when he asks for bread, or a serpent if he asks for
fish, He asks since we know how to give things to our children, how much more
will our Heavenly Father give us good things when we ask Him for them (Mt 7:
7–9). Because He is going to the Father, He tells us, everything that we ask the
Father for in His name, He, Jesus, will do it, so that His Father may be glorified
in Him. Emphatically, he insists: "If you shall ask me anything in my name, that
I will do" (Mt 14: 13–14).

Interestingly, Jesus also explains to us that when two or more agree together in
prayer, "concerning anything whatsoever," they shall ask, and His Father will
grant their petitions (Mt 18: 19). When we want our prayers answered, we
should find someone to enter into agreement with us as we pray in Jesus name.

When Jesus was in Nazareth, the people there could not understand how He
could work miracles and have great wisdom, since he was a native of the town
and they thought they knew Him and His family (Mt 15: 34). Sadly the Scripture says that He did not work many miracles there, because of their unbelief. To
them, He was just the carpenter's son (Mt: 15: 35–58. The disciples also had
problems as they tried to follow Jesus' teaching and heal the sick. Once when
they tried to cast out a demon and were unable to, they came to Jesus and asked
why they could not rid the person of the evil spirit. Responding that it was
because of their unbelief, Jesus told them that some evil spirits are cast out only
by prayer and fasting (Mt 17: 20). If our prayers are not being answered, we
should try fasting when we pray.

The apostles continued the healing ministry of Jesus after He ascended to His
Father and the Holy Spirit came to them on Pentecost. Shortly after they received
the Holy Spirit, Peter and John went to the temple to pray. As they were about to
enter the temple through the Beautiful Gate, they saw a man of approximately
forty years of age lying there, begging because he had been lame from birth.
When the man asked the apostles for alms, Peter said, "Look upon us." Hoping
to receive money from them, the man did as he was told. "Silver and gold, I have
none," said Peter "but what I have, I give you. In the name of Jesus Christ of
Nazareth, arise, and walk" (Acts 3: 6). As he took the man by his right hand,
Peter lifted him up and strength came into him. Jumping up, the man stood and

walked. Then leaping with joy and praising God, he went into the temple with Peter and John, causing all the people who witnessed his healing to be filled with wonder and amazement. A large crowd soon gathered around them where they were in Solomon's Porch. Peter seeing a good opportunity to preach the gospel of Christ to them said:

> "You men of Israel, why wonder you at this? Or why look you upon us, as if by our strength or power we had made this man to walk? The God of Abraham, and the God of Isaac, and the God of Jacob, the God of our fathers, has glorified his Son Jesus, whom you indeed delivered up and denied before the face of Pilate, when he judged he should be released." (Acts 3: 1–17)

Because many were converted by seeing the miracle and hearing Peter preach, the officers of the temple and the Sadducees tried to silence the apostles by forbidding them to preach in the name of Jesus. Emboldened by the indwelling Holy Spirit, Peter makes it perfectly clear that the miracle was to be attributed to Jesus.

> If we this day are examined concerning the good deed done to the infirm man, by what means he has been made whole, be it known to you all, and to all the people of Israel, that by the name of our Lord Jesus Christ of Nazareth, whom you crucified, whom God hath raised from the dead, even by Him this man stands here before you whole." (Acts 4: 9–10)

Peter left no doubt in their minds as to how the miracle had been achieved. To make himself perfectly clear, he told them: "Neither is there salvation in any other. For there is no other name under heaven given to men, whereby we must be saved" (Acts 4: 12).

Once again we note the relationship between healing and preaching the Word of God. Each is meant to reinforce the other. When the gospel is preached with the power of the Holy Spirit we can fully expect miracles to occur. When miracles occur we can fully expect many people to come to Christ.

The Apostle Philip also had miracles in his ministry—the lame and the paralyzed were cured and evil spirits were cast out (Acts 8: 7–8). In Lydda, Peter healed Eneas who had been paralyzed for eight yeas. He simply said to him: "The Lord Jesus Christ heals you—arise…" (Acts 9: 34). In Joppa, a woman called Tabitha died. Her people washed her and laid her out. When the people of Lydda heard that Peter was in Joppa, not far away, they sent for him. When Peter arrived, they took him to the room with the body of Tabitha where all the people were weeping. After asking them to leave, Peter knelt down and turned to the body and simply said, "Tabitha, arise" (Acts 9: 40). At once she opened her eyes and arose and many people believed in the Lord, because of this miracle. And the Lord Jesus has continued to work miracles of healing ever since.

The Apostle James writes in his epistle the following about healing:

> Is any man sick among you? Let him bring in the priests of the Church and let them pray over him, anointing him with oil in the name of the Lord. And the prayer of faith shall save the sick man, and the Lord shall raise him up: and if he be in sins, they shall be forgiven him. (Jas 5: 15–16)

But James also says we have to ask in faith without wavering, because if we waver we are like a wave on the sea that the wind blows about to and fro (Jas 1: 6).

In conclusion, let us remember that the healing of sickness and disease will take place wherever the power of the Lord Jesus Christ is present. If we can find Him, we can be healed. He is the same yesterday, today, and tomorrow; He does not change. We have to believe that He can heal us and that He wants to heal us. We have seen in this chapter that He has compassion on human infirmities and people have only to ask with faith, believing that they will be healed, in order to call forth His healing power. Since sickness and disease are the result of our human condition as descendants of Adam and Eve, we should strive to get rid of sin in our lives, if we want His healing power to infuse us and transform us. Our prayers are strengthened, if we find someone to pray with us in agreement for our healing. The laying on of hands is an effective way for a Spirit filled person to transmit the healing light of Jesus. If we are ill, we should seek out followers of Jesus to lay their hands on us and pray that we might be restored to health.

Once one has been healed, the best way to live free of sickness and disease to stay close to Jesus, especially by receiving Him in the Eucharist frequently. When we are healed, we are to testify to the wonderful things the Lord has done for us, by telling as many people as possible about them. We note that in the healings He performed when He was in the land of the Bible, the people who were healed approached him reverently, some even on their knees to worship Him, while asking for His healing touch.

"Lord Jesus, You are Life and we are often plagued by sickness and disease, harbingers of death. We come to You that You may give us life and heal us of all our infirmities. We know you want us to be well so that we can serve you all the days of our lives. We believe that You can heal us, that you want to heal, and we thank you for the healing that we know you are even now working in us. We now see ourselves healed and happy, strong and well, resembling the picture You have of us in heaven where You see us already present there with You in glory as we wait for our complete transformation in You. We ask the Father to grant this prayer, in Your name, Lord Jesus, and we pray in the unity of the Holy Spirit. Amen."

Be Free from Envy

Envy is a sin that has been a familiar one down through the ages ever since the Garden of Eden. Christians have dealt with it in many ways. One of the earliest Church writers to treat this matter extensively was St. Thascius Cyprian (ca 200–258), Bishop of Carthage, who was martyred for his faith in Christ in the Decian persecution, approximately twelve years after his conversion to Christianity.

In his treatise "On Jealousy and Envy," he describes these sins as being a "dark and hidden mischief." He writes: "And if anyone closely look into this, he will find that nothing should be more guarded against by the Christian, nothing more carefully watched, than being taken captive by envy and malice, that none, entangled in the blind snares of a deceitful enemy, in that the brother is turned by envy to hatred of his brother, should himself be unwittingly destroyed by his own sword" (3).

From this point of departure, the saint proceeds to seek out the sources and the magnitude of envy and its evils. Relating how Satan was the first one to be destroyed by the sins of jealously and envy, he writes: "He who was sustained in angelic majesty, he who was accepted and beloved of God, when he beheld man made in the image of God, broke forth into jealousy with malevolent envy—not hurling down another by the instinct of his jealousy before he himself was first hurled down by jealousy, captive before he takes captive, ruined before he ruin others" (4). Because of his rampant jealousy and envy, Satan robbed Adam and Eve of their immortality, bringing death into our world.

From the time Adam and Ever were expelled from the Garden of Eden, the Holy Scripture is filled with stories that reveal the jealously and envy of sinful men. To cite just a few, we mention: Cain killed his brother Abel; Esau felt envy and hatred towards Jacob who received their fathers blessing; Joseph's brothers sold him into slavery because of envy; and Saul was enraged because people praised David so highly for killing the giant Goliath.

According to St. Cyprian jealousy and envy are the root of many evils, "the fountain of disasters, the nursery of crimes" (6). Envy gives rise to hatred and jealousy leads to ambition and greed, because when one sees the good things someone else possesses he wants to have them for himself. "But what a gnawing worm of the soul is it, what a plague spot of our thoughts, what a rust of the heart, to be jealous of another, either in respect of his virtue or of his happiness…" (7).

Envy and jealousy are especially insidious sins, because they destroy the one who is guilty of them and wreak havoc on those touched by them. In a homily on 2 Corinthians, St. John Chrysostom, speaking of the horrible effects of jealousy and envy, states:

> We fight one another, and envy arms us against one another. If everyone strives to unsettle the body of Christ, where shall we end up? We are engaged in making Christ's Body a corpse. We declare ourselves members of one and the same organism, yet we devour one another like beasts." (3–4). \

The Holy Scripture also has much to say to condemn envy and jealousy. In the book of Job we read: "Anger indeed kills the foolish, and envy slays the little one" (5: 2). While love is strong as death, jealousy is hard as hell and "the lamps thereof are fire and flames" (Song 8: 6).

St. Paul tells us to eschew envy: "Let us walk honestly, as in the day, not in rioting and drunkenness, not in chambering and impurities, not in contention and envy" (Rom 13: 13). And again he writes: "Let us not be made desirous of vainglory, provoking one another, envying one another" (Gal 5: 26). The Apostle James also attacks envy in the people of God. He writes: "Where envying and contention is, there is inconstancy, and every evil work" (3: 16). He continues: "You covet, and have not; you kill, and envy, and can not obtain. You contend and war, and you have not, because you ask not" (Jas 4: 2). Rather than being jealous and envious of others and what they have, we should pray and ask the Lord to help us grow and advance and for Him to give us the good things we need.

Many of the saints have looked at envy and written about it. St. Gregory of Nyssa finds it to be a worse sin than wrath.

> Let no one imagine that I consider the viciousness of wrath the gravest of the evil produced by hatred. Envy and hypocrisy seem to me much worse diseases than the one just mentioned, since a hidden evil is more dangerous than one that is obvious. In the case of dogs, too, we beware more of those whose fury is not announced in advance by their barking, so that their attack does not seem immanent, but who, under a pleasantly gentle appearance wait for us to be unsuspecting and off our guard. Such is the disease of envy and hypocrisy; it is cherished secretly in the depth of the heart, like a hidden fire, while externally everything is made to look deceptively like friendship. It is like a fire that is hidden under chaff. For a time it smolders inside and burns only what lies

near; the flame does not flare up visibly, only a biting smoke penetrates, because it is so vigorously compressed from within. But if it meets with some gust of wind, it is rekindled into a bright open flame. Thus envy, too, consumes the heart from within like fire that is kept down by a pile of chaff. (*Beatitudes* 162)

Gregory explains that one can conceal envy for a time, but it will be observed by the telltale looks the one guilty of envy makes when the envied person meets with some misfortune, because he will rejoice over the envied man's sorrow. Furthermore, he explains that there are certain symptoms of envy that betray the one guilty of it. The one who envies find no pleasure in life, but groans inwardly and rejoices to hear the envied person slandered. He compounds his evil with hypocrisy by pretending to be a friend of the one envied and offers him wishes for happiness, but silently is thinking the contrary.

The Catechism of the Catholic Church reminds us that envy is a capital sin, for many sins proceed from it and when one wishes a neighbor serious harm, it becomes a mortal sin (2539). St. Augustine describes it aptly when he refers to it as "the diabolic sin" (*De catechizandis rudibus* 315–316).

One of the great masters of the spiritual life, Adolphe Tanquerey, S.S., S.D, describes envy as both a capital sin and a passion. The passion consists in the sadness the envious person experiences because of someone's good fortune. When people are envious, Tanquerey explains, they tend to be saddened over another person's blessings and often desire that the blessed person be deprived of his benefits. We can spot an envious person by the anguish that he exhibits when someone else is praised and he immediately begins to criticize that person. His pride is devastated by the other person's happiness. Envy, of course, stems from pride which is the mother of all sins.

According to Tanquerey, envy is a mortal sin by its very nature, because it is against charity which demands that we rejoice in the blessings of others. The more important the qualities that we envy, the more serious is our sin. Quoting St. Thomas, Tanquerey states that being envious of someone's spiritual progress is a very grave sin, if one fully consents to it.

Envy is especially evil, says Tanquerey, because it stirs up feelings of hatred for those we envy and often leads to our denigrating them or wishing them harm. It also leads to dissention and discord. Because jealousy and envy often incite people to work immoderately for wealth and honors, it leads them to overwork and do things of a questionable nature. Because of envy, many people lose their peace of soul and live in perpetual anguish.

The remedies Tanquerey suggests for envy are of two kinds, positive and negative. The negative remedies consist in refusing to entertain jealous and envious thoughts and crushing them as one would a snake. We can do this by turning our thoughts to more appropriate topics. Tanquerey suggests the following as a positive means of dealing with jealousy and envy:

> If it be the virtues of another that we envy, instead of bearing them envy and jealousy on account of those virtues, as occurs often through the suggestion of the evil one and of self-love, you should unite to the Holy Spirit of Jesus Christ in the Blessed Sacrament, honoring in Him the sources of those virtues, and begging of Him the grace to share and partake therein. You will see how useful and how profitable such practice is to you. (*Spiritual Life* 406)

A second positive way of dealing with jealously and envy is the practice of emulation, by seeking to imitate the virtues of others to make us better, not to put us ahead of someone we envy. To acquire the virtues we proceed, using the proper means, to go about it—work, effort, and the divine gifts. In this way we turn envy into the cultivation of virtue (404–407).

Envy and jealousy are sins that can attack anyone. People in religious life are especially susceptible because they have given up so much to follow Christ that their minds are often employed in comparing themselves to others. It has been said envy is the sin of the clergy. If a priest does something out of the ordinary that his fellow priests are not able to do, he is putting himself in a position to be envied, because he does not adhere to clerical culture that demands conformity and uniformity. Rather than praising God, for the grace given to the priest who has a special task to do in the kingdom, they berate him and rejoice at any misfortune that might befall him. Envy is an especially insidious and odious sin because it causes the envious to anguish over the successes of others and robs them of their peace of soul. Envy can be rooted out with the help of God's grace, by frequenting the sacrament of penance and confessing any jealousy or envy we might feel and resolving to eradicate them from our hearts. The advice for overcoming jealousy and envy that St. Cyprian gave eighteen hundred years ago is still very valid and appropriate today.

> Cast away all that malice wherewith you were before held fast, and be reformed to the way of eternal life in the footsteps of salvation. Tear out from your breast thorns and thistles that the Lord's seed may enrich you with a fertile produce, that the divine and spiritual cornfield may abound to the plentiful harvest. Cast out the poison of gall, cast out the virus of discord. Let the

mind which the malice of the serpent had infected be purged; let all bitterness which had settled within be softened by the sweetness of Christ. Love those whom you previously had hated; favor those whom you envy with unjust disparagements. Imitate good men, if you are able to follow them; but if you are not able to follow them, at least rejoice with them, and congratulate those who are better than you. (17)

The remedy for the sin of envy is to accept God's gifts that He bestows on everyone. Envy for material things is foolish, because material things will all disappear in time. Envy of spiritual blessings is a far worse sin, because they are God's special gifts.

"Dear Lord Jesus, we are sorry for every jealous or envious thought we have ever had. Please free us from this terrible evil. May we always show charity to everyone in our thoughts, words, and deeds. We forgive all who have mistreated us because of their envy. Have mercy on them and forgive them and teach them to be charitable. Amen."

Be Free from Want

When God created the world he did not create it in a state of perfection. Its ultimate perfection has not yet been reached. By His Providence, He guides creation toward that perfection that He has planned for it. The First Vatican Council in the document "On God the Creator of All Things," speaks of the Providence of God in caring for His creation:

> Everything that God has brought into being He protects and governs by His providence, which reaches from one end of the earth to the other and orders all things well [11]. All things are open and laid bare to His eyes [12], even those, which will be brought about by the free activity of creatures. (4)

God's providence is difficult for the mind of man to fathom. No doubt we are all familiar with the adage, "Man proposes and God disposes." The book of Proverbs tells us that men have many plans, but God's purposes will prevail (19: 21). This should be comforting to know, because no matter how hard our enemies or the enemies of Christ try to thwart God's plans for our lives and our happiness, they will not be able to do so. God's purposes *will* prevail.

Throughout the Old Testament, we can see God's Providence at work. A very good example of His loving Providence at work in human lives can be found in the story of Joseph and his brothers who sold him into slavery in Egypt, because of their jealousy and envy of him, lying to their father saying he had been devoured by a wild beast.

When great famine came upon the land and the brothers were in dire need of food, they went down into Egypt because they had learned that Egypt had corn for sale, never dreaming that the brother they had sold into slavery had become the governor of Egypt. It was because of Joseph's correctly interpreting Pharaoh's dreams that corn had been stored away in times of plenty, so that it was available in time of famine. Impressed by Joseph's wisdom, the Egyptians believed his knowledge came from a divine source and for this reason they raised him to the position of honor as governor. When the brothers appeared before Joseph to buy corn, he recognized them, but they did not know him. When he finally does reveal his identity to them, he tells them:

> "Be not afraid, and let it not seem to you a hard case that you sold me into these countries, for God sent me before you into Egypt for your preservation. For it is two years since the famine began to be upon the land, and five years more remain, wherein there can be neither plowing nor reaping. And God sent me before, that you may be preserved upon the earth, and may have food to live." (Ge 45: 5–5)

Joseph clearly recognizes God's providence at work in all their lives. Accepting what has happened to him as part of God's plan to save His people, he does not show resentment to his brothers, rather he tells them: "You thought evil against me, but God turned it into good, that He might exalt me, as at present you see, and might save many people" (Ge 50: 20). Is this not an example of what St. Paul says is true? "And we know that all things work together for good to them that love God, to them who are called according to his purpose" (Rom 8: 28). God took the evil deed that the brothers did in selling Joseph into slavery and telling their father that a beast had devoured him and turned it into good for all of them.

Still the evil deed of the brothers was a heinous offense. Why is there evil in the world? Why did God not create a world free from evil? The *Catechism of the Catholic Church* answers this question as follows:

> But why did God not create a world so perfect that no evil could exist in it? With infinite power God could always create something better. But with infinite wisdom and goodness, God freely willed to create a world "in a state of journeying" toward its ultimate perfection. In God's plan this process of becoming involves the appearance of certain beings and the disappearance of others, the existence of the more perfect alongside the less perfect, both constructive and destructive forces of nature. With physical good there exists also *physical evil*. He permits it, however, because he respects the freedom of his creatures and, mysteriously, knows how to derive good from it. (310)

We can also see the workings of Providence in the life of God's people when after they left Egypt and wandered for forty years in the desert, the Lord fed them with manna from heaven, which appeared every morning except on the Sabbath. Although there exist a number of things today in the Middle East that bear the name of manna, none of them are the same as the manna that the Lord provided. Not only did He give them manna, but also to satisfy their hunger for meat, the Lord sent quail to where His people were so that they might be satisfied.

Miraculous food also occurred in the life of Elijah, the prophet, who told Ahab that it would not rain for years. The Lord sent Elijah to a brook called Cherith, where He told Elijah that He had commanded ravens to feed him. Holy Scripture records that the ravens brought him bread and meat in the morning and again in the evening day after day. When the brook ran dry and Elijah was no longer able to drink its water, the Lord directed him to go to Zarephath, where He had commanded a woman to feed Elijah.

When Elijah arrived at Zarephath, seeing the widow at the gate of the city gathering sticks, he called to her: "Give me a little water in a vessel, that I may drink" (1 Ki 17: 10). When she started to do as he requested, he called after her, "Bring me also, I beseech you, a morsel of bread in your hand" (1 Ki 17: 11). "As the Lord God lives," she replied "I have no bread, but only a handful of meal in a pot, and a little oil in a cruse. Behold I am gathering two sticks that I may go in and dress it, for me and my son, that we may eat it and die." Elijah told her:

> "Fear not, but go, and do as you have said, but first make for me of the same meal a little hearth cake, and bring it to me, and after make for yourself and your son. For thus says the Lord, the God of Israel: 'The pot of meal shall not waste, nor the cruse of oil be diminished, until the day wherein the Lord will give rain upon the face of the earth.'" (1 Ki 17: 13–14)

The woman did as she was told and the scant provisions of oil and meal did not run out, but continued to sustain her, her son, and Elijah as long as was needed. It was providential that the prophet was staying in her house, because her son became sick, "and the sickness was very grievous, so that there was no breath left in him" (1Ki 17: 17). In her depression the widow cried out to Elijah: "What have I to do with you, you man of God? Are you come to me that my iniquities should be remembered, and that you should kill my son?" "Give me your son," replied Elijah taking the boy to the room where he stayed and, putting the lad on his bed, cried out to the Lord: "O Lord my God, let the soul of this child, I beseech You, return into his body" (1Ki 17: 21). Elijah was able to restore the boy alive to his mother.

The Old Testament speaks much of the wonderful loving Providence of God. Consider the psalm that begins "The Lord is my shepherd." The psalmist David knew well how God provides for His people. "I shall want nothing," he proclaims (Ps 22: 1). The psalmist delights in singing the glory of God's Providence.

> Many are the afflictions of the just, but out of them all will the Lord deliver them. The Lord keeps all their bones, not one of them shall be broken. The

rich have wanted, and have suffered hunger, but they that seek the Lord shall not be deprived of any good. The death of the wicked is very evil, and they that hate the just shall be guilty. The Lord will redeem the souls of his servants, and none of them that trust in Him shall offend. (Ps 33: 11, 20–26).

In Psalm 36, we read, "Trust in the Lord, and do good, and dwell in the land and you shall be fed with its riches" (36: 3) Psalm ninety is especially beautiful in the way it describes the protection God gives to his faithful ones.

> He that dwells in the aid of the most High, shall abide under the protection of the God of Jacob. He shall say to the Lord: You are my protector and my refuge; in Him will I trust, for He has delivered me from the snare of the hunters and from the sharp word. He will overshadow you with his shoulders and under His wings you shall not be afraid of the terror of the night, of the arrow that flies in the day, of the business that walks about in the dark, of invasion, or of the noonday devil. A thousand shall fall at thy side, and ten thousand at thy right hand, but it shall not come nigh to you. But you shall consider with your eyes and shall see the reward of the wicked. Because, You, O Lord, are my hope. You have made the Most High your refuge. There shall no evil come to you, nor shall the scourge come near your dwelling, for He has given His angels charge over you, to keep you in all your ways. In their hands, they shall bear you up, lest you dash your foot against a stone. You shall walk upon the asp and the basilisk and you shall trample under foot the lion and the dragon. Because he hoped in Me, I will deliver him. I will protect him because he has known my name. He shall cry to Me, and I will hear him. I am with him in tribulation. I will deliver him and I will glorify him. I will fill him with length of days, and I will show him my salvation.

We truly have nothing to fear, absolutely nothing, for our God is with us and although it seems that evil things are happening to us, we are confident, because we know that He will draw good from every evil. Our Divine Lord tells us not to resist evil, but if someone strikes us on one cheek to turn the other cheek so he can strike it also (Mt 5: 39). We are not to worry, Christ tells us. "Therefore I say unto you, take no thought for your life, what you shall eat, or what you shall drink, nor yet for your body, what you shall put on. Is not the life more than meat, and the body than raiment? (Mt 6: 25). Pointing out to us that our Heavenly Father feeds the birds of the air, He asks us if we are not much better than they. He reminds us of the beauty of the lilies of the field, saying that even Solomon was not as glorious as they. If God clothes the grass, will He not much more clothe us?

Wherefore, if God so clothe the grass of the field, which today is, and tomorrow is cast into the oven, shall He not much more clothe you, O you of little faith? Therefore take no thought saying" What shall we eat? Or, What shall we drink? Or Wherewithal shall we be clothed? For after all these things do the Gentiles seek. For your Heavenly Father knows that you have need of all these things. But seek first the kingdom of God and His righteousness and all these things shall be added unto you. Take therefore no thought for the morrow, for the morrow shall take thought for the things of itself. Sufficient unto the day is the evil thereof. (Mt 6: 30–34)

Following in the footsteps of Christ, St. Paul had great faith in the loving Providence of God. To the Philippians, he wrote, "And may my God supply all your wants, according to His riches in glory in Christ Jesus" (Php 4: 19). To the Corinthians he wrote: "And God is able to make all grace abound in you, that you always, having all sufficiency in all things, may abound to every work" (2 Cor 9: 8). Out future is glorious; Christ is our life and our way to the Father and to heaven. He supplies everything we need to arrive safely into the realms of glory. When we overcome the adversities that we encounter in this life, He will give us the Morning Star; He will give us Himself, wiping away every tear and filling us with gladness and joy.

"Lord Jesus, we know that you supply all our needs according to your riches in glory. We thank you for guiding us on our way and in your loving Providence, providing everything we need to arrive safely to heaven and the vision of You, when we shall behold you face to face. When we are discouraged and evil seems to be attacking us from all sides, we will remember that you take all evil and derive good from it and that everything, absolutely everything, works together for good for those who love You and are called according to your purposes. Amen"

Set Your Heart Free

Sometimes the problems of daily life seem to be insurmountable. At times, not even when we repent and ask for forgiveness and forgive others do we seem to achieve inner peace. Our hearts feel cold and empty and have no joy. What is the problem? What can we do about it?

The trouble is that many of us are spiritual dwarfs who do not know how to confront our problems and manage our happiness. We need to advance in the spiritual life. Many Christians are worn out, tired, defeated, depressed, and do not know how to find the joy Christ promises those who love Him. When people phone the rectory it is usually because something is wrong. Few, if any, call to tell how God has blessed them, and if they do perhaps they will not find anyone willing to listen to their good news. People spend their lives confessing the bad, the ugly, and the accidents, instead of praising God for the wonderful things He is constantly doing in their lives. We have all been blessed abundantly; everything in the Christian life is grace. We need to rejoice in our blessings and learn to deal effectively with our problems.

When we have a problem, we need to recall the words of St. Paul: "I can do all things in Him who strengthens me" (Php 4: 13). We need not be afraid, for we have the best protector in the world, Jesus Christ, "because greater is He that is in you, than he that is in the world" (1 Jn 4: 4). Acknowledging this, what do we do with our problems? Put them in the hands of Jesus. We do not look at our problem and pain, but keep our eyes on Christ glorified who will give us the power and strength to be victorious in every situation. We just do what we have to, never changing our course of action in moments of crisis or tribulation. Above all we praise God, giving thanks to Him in every moment of our lives, singing His praises joyfully, remembering, "the joy of the Lord is our strength" (Neh 8: 10). Our lives might be menaced by danger and death, but we can always advance in the name of Jesus Christ. In Him we can be happy and content.

We need to learn to deal with the bad things that happen to us and to take advantage of the good. This means accepting the will of God completely. The Lord will allow events that are meant to purify us. We will have to submit to suffering sometimes and learn how to manage it, because God lets us all go through periods of purification from time to time. Occasionally, we have problems that have no human solution. For example, someone we love might die or we might endure a financial catastrophe that seems to be more than we can manage. Why is that? There are no simple answers, but we can always let our hearts be purified as we manage our adversities.

Sometimes the routine monotony of daily life becomes almost insupportable. Every day we get up, dress, go to work so that one day resembles every other and we suffer from boredom. How can we deal with this? When one lives in Christ, the monotonous life because charged with His presence and becomes interesting, rewarding, and even exciting.

We encounter disagreeable situations. For example, sometimes we have to work in the same place with people who do not like us. Or perhaps we have to live in the same house with someone who is incompatible, or even worse, has a basic antipathy toward us. How do we handle this? When there is no solution, we embrace the cross and breathe a sigh, praying, "Your will be done, not mine."

No matter how difficult our situation might seem, God can transform it into blessing. The Holy Scripture assures us: "And we know that to them that love God, all things work together unto good, to such as, according to his purpose, are called to be saints" (Rom 8: 28) We need to realize that God knows what is good for us. He is a good Father who loves us and cares for us in every situation. We accept His will just exactly as He wishes, when He wishes, and for as long as He wishes. Embracing His will gives Jesus the key to all we have.

At times, we need to experience progressive abnegation. This involves doing things that are not pleasant and to our liking, because the Lord puts them in our lives. An abnegated person follows Christ saying, "I am not here because of all you give me, but because I love you!" Such people have a great impact on society. They know that to love is to surrender and to make a decision to do good to someone. It also means to live free of resentment and other negative emotions. This is the highest degree of loving.

Many weary people live with resentment in their hearts; because of this it is impossible for them to be joyful. Since God wants us to be happy mentally as well as physically, we need to be healed of all sadness, resentment, and bad memories, because they cause many kinds of ailments—ulcers, insomnia, anxiety, and depression, among other things.

To be cured of all these miseries, we must first really want to be healed.

The Lord Jesus wants us to be cured of them now, effectively and completely. He tells us: "The thief comes not, but for to steal, and to kill, and to destroy. I am come that they may have life, and may have it more abundantly" (Jn 10: 10).

Sadness, pessimism, depression, and anxiety are all weapons of the enemy and are meant to destroy our lives. Joy, happiness, and self-control are gifts of God to make our lives beautiful and worthwhile. Unfortunately, many of us have made our religion boring and sad. Our Lord wants us to rejoice and the Holy Scripture insists: "Rejoice, again I say rejoice!" (Php 4: 4).

Happiness is a vital part of the Christian life. If we are sad or bitter all the time we are not good Christians, because we lack the joy of the Lord. Furthermore, we are not to worry. St Paul says: "Be solicitous of nothing; but in everything, by prayer and supplication, with thanksgiving, let your petitions be made known to God" (Php 4: 6). We are to give thanks at all times, not just when things are going well. We must realize that everything we have is God's gift to us—our eyesight, hearing, life itself. Let us give thanks to Him every moment of our lives.

We who are in Christ are closely united to Him and we should receive His gift of peace into our hearts. What do we have to do to get peace and interior tranquility? First, we place all our problems in the hands of God and leave them there. Second, we must forgive all our enemies, all those who have offended us. Finally, we must love others as Jesus does.

Some problems can be resolved while others have no solution. After putting our problems in God's hands, we must turn to His light to find answers, relying on the gifts of the Holy Spirit to guide us. Next we must forgive just as Christ forgave on the cross when he said, "Father, forgive them, for they know not what they do" (Lu 23: 34).

To have a full and joyful life, we have to love those who surround us, for the key to happiness is found precisely when we do that. We cannot be happy without love. Love blesses, cures, and heals all wounds. Let us heed the words of the Apostle John: " Dearly beloved, let us love one another, for charity is of God. And every one that loves, is born of God, and knows God" (1 Jn 4: 7). When we love, we dwell in Him and He in us. "And this commandment we have from God, that he, who loves God, love also his brother" (1Jn 4: 21).

In sum, our ability to achieve inner peace depends on trusting everything to God, forgiving all, loving all, and receiving the Lord's grace setting us free to rejoice.

From time to time, all of us have felt inadequate to confront the things that life sends our way. However, there are some people who feel constantly inadequate; they have what is known as an inferiority complex and suffer from a bad self-image that can be healed.

Since the Lord tells us that we are to love our neighbor as we love ourselves, we each need to ask ourselves the question, "Do I love myself?" Loving one's self is not selfishness. Rather it is a necessary precursor to loving other people. If we do not have the proper love for self, it is impossible to love someone else. However, if we love ourselves in an egotistical manner, our love for our neighbor will not be the kind of love the Lord is asking for us to have. He wants us to love with His love—to love selflessly—entering into His love for us so that we can share it with others.

The question naturally arises. How can we develop a good self-image so that we can love our neighbors and ourselves, as God wants us to? To do this we must overcome our feelings of rejection, our guilt complexes, and our human perfectionism.

Our entire lives we all—some people more, others less—have had to deal with rejection. We have all known those who say we are useless. Perhaps a parent has told us in moments of discouragement, "Child, you are not good for anything. You'll never make it in life." Perhaps we were made to feel inferior because of some personal characteristic. If we are male, perhaps we were a disappointment to our father because we did not have the athletic ability he had. Or if we are female, perhaps our parents wanted a son. There are countless reasons why a person can be made to feel rejected and inferior.

When we went to school, perhaps our clothes were not as nice as the clothing of the other children. Perhaps we did not have as much money to spend as the others did. Perhaps we were not invited by other children to play or go to parties. Perhaps when we got older and married our father-in-law and mother-in-law did not like us and thought we were not good enough to marry their son or daughter. Whatever the cause of our feelings of rejection, the Bible offers solutions to improving our bad self-image.

Being rejected tends to make us feel guilty. There are some people that no matter how often they go to confession they still feel guilty. This is regrettable and must be dealt with, because a guilt complex makes it impossible for us to love our neighbors, and ourselves, as God wants.

When we are young, our parents and our teachers tell us that we must do certain things, transmitting to us a set of values that become so deeply entrenched in us that we feel good about ourselves if we hold to them. Conversely if we do not live up to these societal values, we have a bad opinion of ourselves.

We also have strictures our consciences put upon us and which are based on the Word of God, indicating what is good moral behavior and what is not. If we do not follow our consciences, we do not feel pleased with ourselves. Rather we are displeased and unhappy.

A problem can arise here if we have not formed our consciences correctly, according to the teaching of the Church. If we have a properly formed conscience, when we repent and confess our sins, we know that God has forgiven them forever and we don't think about them anymore. If a person continues to feel guilty after having repented and confessed, he is not following Christ's teaching and is suffering from a guilt complex. The conscience is meant to reform our lives to conform to Christian principles. In some people the conscience does not work correctly.

Some people are perfectionists and are never satisfied with what they or anyone else ever does. For example, there are some people who say they can never forgive themselves for having done some particular thing. These people are very proud, not devout. A person who keeps feeling guilty after having been pardoned is a proud person who needs to accept God's forgiveness.

What does God say to those who have guilt feelings? What does God have to say to those who are perfectionists? "I have loved you with an eternal love." We must learn to love others and ourselves as God has loved us.

There are many man-made systems designed to make people happy—for example, transcendental meditation, yoga, or mind control, or ways of positive thinking. None of them can bring true happiness; there is only one way for us to be happy and that is in following the Lord Jesus Christ and believing His words of eternal life with the Holy Spirit dwelling in our hearts. Each one of us is a unique creation of God, and He only possesses the keys to our happiness.

When people feel inferior and say that they are not good and have dirt under their fingernails, we respond, "Just as you are, the Lord Jesus loves you and died for you on the cross." God loves us just the way we are. We do not have to change to come to Him; we come to Him just as we are and He will change us to be the people He wants us to be and we want to become. Just as we are, the Holy Spirit has chosen us to be His temples and He wants us to live happily and joyfully in His love.

Since we are the children of God, who can possibly reject us and make us feel inferior? When we have the Holy Spirit and Jesus dwelling in our hearts, it doesn't matter if people do not like us and reject us. We are capable people. We can do all things through Christ who gives us the strength.

The first thing we can do to give ourselves a new self-image is to realize the great love God has for each of us. We must accept His plan for our happiness and joy. If someone tries to make us inferior by comparing us to someone else, we refuse to be compared with anyone. Each of us is a unique creation of God. And if someone does something to make us feel inferior, we will say to ourselves, "It doesn't matter to me. I am a child of God." Each one of us is an exclusive model made for God Himself. Since God made us, we must be of value. We are not ugly or worthless. We are treasured children of the Heavenly Father and since He created us there must be something marvelous about us.

We do not need transcendental meditation or yoga, because we have the Word of God with the beautiful plan He has designed for our lives—a plan to make us happy and to glorify us. In the Word of God we will find everything we need to live in His mercy and happiness.

To obtain a good self-image we need to consider that "God sent not his Son into the world to condemn the world; but that the world through him might be saved" (Jn 3: 17). To get the full impact of this, we need to insert our own names into this verse.

God dos not desire the death of a sinner, but rather that he be converted and live. Some people think that God is just waiting to catch them and send them to hell. God never sends anyone to hell; people send themselves there.

Yes, hell exists, because Jesus says it does. But Jesus has a plan of salvation, not a plan of condemnation. Salvation begins in this life the moment we say, "Jesus Christ, I want to walk with you. I want you to be the Lord of my life. I want my name to be written in the book of life and I want to go to the realms of glory to be with you forever." This is a prayer Jesus always loves to answer.

The power of Jesus is within us. The gifts of the Holy Spirit enlighten us. "Behold, what manner of love the Father hath bestowed upon us, that we should be called the sons of God; therefore the world knows us not, because it knew him not" (1 Jn 3: 1). Since God calls us sons and daughters and invites us to His banquet at the Holy Eucharist and to the wedding feast of the Lamb, there must be something good about us. If we were no good, we could not draw near to Jesus Christ, but He loves us and wants us to come to Him.

When we consider the great love of God, as we recall that Jesus has redeemed us by His death on the cross, we need to clear our minds of the denigrating things people have said to us and of our own base feelings about ourselves, and develop a positive identity within. When we feel sure of ourselves and that we are really worth something, we give people the benefit of the doubt, when we think they might be rejecting us. However, if we are certain they are rejecting us, we remember that we are sons and daughters of the Heavenly Father and temples of the Holy Spirit and we simply say, "What does it matter? I am child of the King of Kings and a temple of the Holy Spirit. It just does not matter to me."

When we have reached this point, we are able to love. Love is learned living with the Spirit of God. It is learned at the foot of the cross of Jesus. Only Jesus can heal our bad self-images; only He can free us from the false thinking of the world. We who are in Christ are new creations and the old have passed away. Only by becoming new creatures in Christ can we get rid of the little things in our hearts that impede us, as we let Jesus heal us of our bad self-images and self-love. Once He has healed us, we can rejoice in the great gifts God has given us, realizing that all we have is His gift and He has no obligation to give us any gifts or even another minute of time.

Enemies who attack us trouble some of us. We must always remember that Jesus Christ is much bigger and greater than every enemy, for the Scripture says: "Greater is He who is within you than he who is in the world" (1 Jn 4: 4). He can give us the victory over anything or anyone that attacks us or disturbs us. However, sometimes the Lord tests us and our loyalty to Him by letting us have tribulations. The Apostle Peter wrote of this: "Wherein you shall greatly rejoice, if now you must be for a little time made sorrowful in divers temptations: That the trial of your faith (much more precious than gold which is tried by the fire) may be found unto praise and glory and honor at the appearing of Jesus Christ" (1 Pe 1: 6–7).

The Lord always takes evil and turns it into blessing for those who love Him (Rom 8: 28). If we have a dread disease, Jesus can either cure us in this life or not, but when we get to heaven He will heal us totally. Nevertheless, it is possible to feel joyful even if we have cancer and do not feel well, if we ask Jesus for joy. There are people who are happy for a time, but they are not joyful, because joy comes into a heart that is in communion with God. When He gives us joy no one can take it away from us.

In our western society, we put much emphasis on material things—the kind of car we drive, the brand of clothing we wear. These things are not really important. What really counts is what is in our hearts. However, we cannot read people hearts to know what their intentions are when they do something.

Some women want to live like princesses and are overly concerned about their outward appearance. The beautiful woman is the one whose heart is filled with the love of God. The handsome man is one that is filled with the pardon and grace that comes from the power of God. If we have incorruptible beauty in our hearts, people will notice that our hearts are overflowing with the love, truth, and the joy of Jesus Christ. We will not need to seek exterior adornment, if our hearts are adorned with the spiritual gifts of God. A woman who is adorned with God's grace does not need a lot of cosmetics and jewelry to be attractive.

The Lord expects us to find reward in our activities. For the Christian, working is not a punishment but a way to develop ourselves. We cannot be idle, for an idle mind is the devil's workshop. Even the handicapped should be permitted to do things, because we all need to feel useful.

Basically there are two steps to obtaining a good self-image and living at peace with all. First we need to remember the great love God has for us, such as expressed by Isaiah. "Since thou became honorable in my eyes, you are glorious: I have loved you, and I will give men for you, and people for your life" (Is 43: 4) "And every one that calls upon my name, I have created him for my glory, I have formed him, and made him" (Is 43: 7).

We need to repeat this to ourselves when we wake up in the mornings. We must be without fear, breathing freely. Another Bible verse that we can repeat is this: "Yes, I have loved you with everlasting love, therefore have I drawn you, taking pity on you" (Jer 31: 3) It doesn't matter what is happening in our lives or how impossible the difficulties.

The second step in getting a good self-image is to realize that we can do all things in Him who strengthens us" (Php 4: 13). If we feel we have no hope, we can find hope in Jesus. If we think no one loves us, we can find love in Christ. If we are worried about what will become of us, we are assured that our future will be glorious, as Christ promises. We have nothing to fear. "For God has not given us the spirit of fear: but of power, and of love, and of sobriety" (2 Ti 1: 7).

If we ask Him, the Lord will give us wisdom to solve our problems as the Holy Spirit even gives us the words to speak, if we ask for His guidance. Through Christ we will be more than conquerors when we are attacked. "Let your manners be without covetousness, contented with such things as you have, for he has said, 'I will not leave you, neither will I forsake you.' So that we may confidently say: The Lord is my helper. I will not fear what man shall do to me" (Heb 13: 5–6)

If God is for us, who can destroy us? We can save our marriages, our homes, and our children. Christ is our defender when we are under attack. We are not afraid, because Christ defends us, so that when people attack us we bless them. We reap what we sow. If we are kind, gentle, and loving to others, they will be that way toward us.

The third step in getting a good self-image is acquiring a humble attitude. May people see the beauty of God in us as we use our gifts for the glory of God. When things do not seem to be going right, we pray and claim the promises of God.

The Heart of Jesus is always open to us and ready to heal us. The Lord invites us to come to Him. "Come unto me, all you that labor, and are burdened, and I will refresh you" (Mt 11: 28) When we are sad, troubled, or depressed, we draw near to the Heart of Jesus, our great refuge, putting everything in His healing Heart.

"Lord Jesus, We give you our hearts; take them in your hands and put them in your healing Heart. Thank you for receiving us and putting our hearts in Your Heart. May Your Precious Blood wash away our sins and Your love ease all our pains. Our hearts are renewed in Your Heart. You are our refuge of liberty, mercy, healing, and refreshment. Lord, pass your healing hands over our lives and hearts. We thank You. We desire always to live in peace with everyone. We place in Your Heart all those who have ever wounded us and all whom we have hurt. We entrust to Your heart all our friends and loved ones who are in pain. Please Lord, put Your healing hands on every situation in our lives that needs to be healed. Heal our memories of past wrongs and suffering. We know all is possible with You. We are renewed in You. Bless us always. Bathe us in Your love and enrich us with all spiritual gifts. Set our hearts free, that we may love and serve you all the days of our lives and live with you in glory for all eternity. Amen."

Be Free from Error

When we set out for the heavenly city and the eternal weight of glory we hope to attain, we must make sure we are traveling the road that will take us there. No doubt we have all had the experience of trying to reach a destination and getting lost and wandering in circles until we found a road map or someone to direct us. When embracing the spiritual life, we need to be directed in the way to go or we might get lost, or, at best encounter, many hazards or detours.

The Church has been directing her members in the paths of holiness for the past two thousand years. One has only to consider the exceedingly great number of canonized saints to realize the truth of this statement. St. Francis de Sales (1567–1622), a holy priest and Doctor of the Church who guided many people to God, insists on the need to find a good guide:

> If you would really tread the paths of the devout life, seek some holy man to guide and conduct you. This is the precept of precepts, says the devout Avila [Saint Teresa],—seek as you will, you can never so surely discover God's Will as through the channel of humble obedience so universally taught and practiced by all the Saints of olden time." (*Intro* Ch IV)

Expanding on this observation, St. Francis de Sales insists that we need a faithful friend who will help us and guide us "thereby guarding us against the deceits and snares of the Evil One." Such a friend will shield us from evil and affirm the good that we do, and when we fall, he will raise us up again so that we will not be permanently cast down. A truly humble person will find a guide if s/he prays and asks God to supply a good holy one, for God will send such a person, even an angel from heaven, if necessary.

Once we have found such a guide, St. Francis says we are to give him our "hearty confidence mingled with sacred reverence."

> In a word, such a friendship should be strong and sweet; altogether holy, sacred, divine and spiritual. And with such an aim, choose one among a thousand, Avila says; —and I say among ten thousand, for there are fewer than one would think capable of this office. He must needs be full of love, of wisdom

and of discretion; for if either of these three be wanting there is danger. But once more I say, seek such help of God, and when you have found it, bless His Holy Name; be steadfast, seek no more, but go on simply, humbly and trustfully, for you are safe to make a prosperous journey." (Ch IV)

It is even more difficult today in the twenty-first century to find a good spiritual guide than when St. Francis wrote *The Introduction to the Devout Life,* over three hundred years ago. One of the main reasons for this is the New Age milieu in which we live with their ideas flooding our society. Unfortunately, there are priests and religious, as well as ministers in almost every Christian denomination, who have accepted New Age thought and practice and are teaching it in the churches and parochial schools. The Holy Scripture warns us that such times would come. "For there shall be a time, when they will not endure sound doctrine, but, according to their own desires, they will heap to themselves teachers, having itching ears" (2 Ti 4: 3). Down through the centuries, there have been those with "itching ears" who have abandoned the sound teachings of the Church and embraced false teachings such as Gnosticism, which even today is one of the sources of New Age thought.

To understand a bit about New Age, we have to realize that it is not a uniform movement, but a loose network of people around the globe who accept and practice different elements of New Age thought. Many people who accept one element of New Age thought or practice are not necessarily aware of New Age philosophy and that is a deliberate challenge to our culture and our faith. Basic to New Age thought is the belief that existing religions are to vanish from the earth to be replaced by New Age spirituality. Early in the third millennium, the Age of Aquarius is supposed to replace the Age of Pisces, the Christian era.

There is very little that is new in New Age thought. Not only have they revived ancient paganism, but they also have borrowed from oriental religions, the psychology of Gustav Jung, pseudoscience, and the counterculture that began at Woodstock in 1969. The musical *Hair* with the song "Aquarius" is one of the New Age icons,

Although, New Age talks about Christ, their idea of Christ is totally different from that of the Catholic Church. To them Jesus is just one Christ of many and all New Agers can become christs too. They do not believe in the existence of sin. Instead, in their view, there is only enlightenment and ignorance. They do not distinguish between good and evil, but only between illumination and ignorance. Consequently, forgiveness is not needed; education is. If there is no sin, there is no need of a redeemer. This approach nullifies the Christian belief in the redemption Jesus Christ obtained for mankind by his death and resurrection.

New Age proponents look forward to a global government and a global spirituality. This leads to grave concerns about the ecology of Mother Earth, aka Gaia, an alternative to Father God of the Bible, and the belief that every plant and animal has as much right to existence as people do. We detect a basic pantheism in New Age thought; there is no personal or transcendent God, for when they speak of god, they mean simply an impersonal energy or force. They stand in fear of a future ecological crisis on the planet. We have all heard stories about how some people have been deprived of the use of their land, because the government insists on protecting the environment there, because some plant or animal faces extinction. There seems to be no concern about whether the landowner faces economic extinction when he can no longer use his property.

When we consider the origins of New Age thought, we find them among intellectuals of the eighteenth and nineteenth centuries in Europe in the esoteric culture of freemasonry, spiritualism, occultism, and theosophy. They regarded nature as a living being, "shot through with networks of sympathy and antipathy, animated by a light and a secret fire which human beings seek to control" ("Jesus Christ the Bearer" 2.3.2) As they saw it, people were to achieve *gnosis*, the epitome of knowledge by following the esoteric teachings that were handed from a master to a disciple.

In 1875, Madame Helene Blavatsky, Russian spiritualist, founded the Theosophical Society with Henry Olcott in New York. Madame Blavatsky, as she is generally known, was very much concerned with the emancipation of women. Consequently, she wanted people to embrace the mother goddess of Hinduism and attacked the "male" deity of the Bible. Following in this tradition, today New Age women are embracing Wicca and feminine spiritually in opposition to what they regard as the patriarchal religions of Judaism and Christianity.

Since Carl Jung and his belief that divinity lurks within every human being and that the path to the cosmos lies in the unconscious mind are well springs from which New Age thought originates, psychology and spirituality merge in New Age philosophy that teaches that one has to find the god that is within in order to realize one's potential. To achieve this, they meditate and resort to mind expanding drugs. One of their key concepts is that of Friedrich Nietzsche that Christianity has prevented the self-fulfillment of humanity.

New Age is powered by the thought of becoming divine and exalts humanity and denies the existence of a God who is transcendent. They regard people as having within them an innate divine spark. The following quotation serves to reflect their ideas:

But we need to make a journey in order fully to understand where we fit into the unity of the cosmos. The journey is psychotherapy, and the recognition of universal consciousness is salvation. There is no sin; there is only imperfect knowledge. The identity of every human being is diluted in the universal being and in the process of successive incarnations." ("Jesus Bearer" 2.3.4.1)

It is not our purpose here to give a full explanation of New Age thought, but merely to indicate its basic antipathy toward Christianity and its incompatibility with Catholic doctrine and practice. The study "Jesus the Water Bearer, of Life: A Christian Reflection on the New Age" concludes that it is not possible to accept some elements of New Age as acceptable to Christians and reject others. "Since the New Age movement makes much of a communication with nature, of cosmic knowledge of a universal good—thereby negating the revealed contents of Christian faith—it cannot be viewed as positive or innocuous." (4)

Since the many facets of New Age thought have permeated our global society in this age of rapid communication, many Catholic people, including priests and religious have bought into it, not realizing that it hopes to replace Christianity with New Age spirituality that is completely and inherently anti Christian. Some people seem to believe that they can take one part of New Age thought without assimilating the rest. This is not possible as the Pontifical Councils cited above affirm. Pope John Paul II warned bishops of these facts in an address to the bishops of Iowa, Kansas, Missouri, and Nebraska May 28, 1993. "New Age ideas often open up a way for themselves in preaching, catechesis, congresses, and retreats, and thus come to influence even practicing Catholics who may not be aware of the incompatibility of those ideas with the faith of the Church" (Carrera 6).

Because we have magnificent and comprehensive teachings on prayer in the writings of the Catholic saints such as St. Teresa of Avila, John of the Cross, St. Bernard, St. Francis de Sales, and countless other holy men and women down through the ages, it is difficult to see why any Catholic would want to embrace a Buddhist prayer technique. Our prayer should be Christ centered and directed to the Heavenly Father in the name of Jesus in the unity of the Holy Spirit.

Unfortunately children in some catechism classes and in some parochial schools are being instructed in New Age practices such as centering prayer. In some dioceses religious sisters are giving classes to laypeople in this oriental way of praying.

Although those who embrace "centering prayer" insist that it is just a method, Archbishop Norberto Rivera Carrera, the ordinary of Mexico City, indicates that it is designed "for guiding the user towards an impersonal absolute." (33a)

Non-Christian forms of meditation are, in reality, practices of deep concentration, not prayer. Through relaxation exercises and the repetition of a "mantra" (sacred word), one strives to submerge himself in the depth of his own "I" in search of the nameless absolute. Christian meditation is essentially different inasmuch as it consists in openness to the transcendent and a relationship with someone who addresses us in a personal, loving dialogue" (33b).

The Archbishop explains that the techniques of "centering prayer" require the practitioner of it to leave the world of senses, imagination and reason "to lose himself in the silence of nothingness." He continues: "Basically, a prayer that disregards the Word of God and Christ's life and example, a prayer that is not a conversation with the Beloved and a commitment to charity, has hardly any place in the life of a Christian" (34).

Commenting that the promoters of New Age spirituality usually insist upon its complete compatibility with Catholic doctrine, they do so in Mexico so as not to offend the large Catholic population that they are trying to lure into their group. "It is not unusual for organizations such as the Great Universal Fraternity and programs such as Silva Mind Control, to name a few, to dress up in a very "Christian" vocabulary and present their beliefs as the ideal complement to Catholicism. Nonetheless, they lead their initiates towards pantheism and the denial of the essence of Christianity" (35).

The experiences of Clare McGrath Merkle, O.C.D.S. confirm the damage that a Catholic can suffer in entering into New Age practices. Encouraged to practice yoga by a Catholic priest who went to a nearby ashram to meditate, sing, and practice yoga every day before his morning Mass, he introduced her to the book *The Course in Miracles.* In a short time, she began to feel that the Catholic Church was not relevant and out of date.

After she began studying Eastern mysticism, and Kriya yoga and practicing daily meditation in *The Course in Miracles*, she began to experience peace in her life, and decided that the Holy Spirit was leading her to leave the Church. She began having out of body experiences. On the night of her twenty-eighth birthday, she believed herself to be with Jesus and her mother and grandmother. When the figure she thought was Jesus took her to a man that looked like an eastern guru, she believed that Jesus was giving her His blessing to leave the Church and practice eastern meditation and yoga. Later she learned that this seeming appearance of Jesus was a deception and that many who become trapped in New Age have similar experiences. Later she decided that it was diabolical.

As she continued praying and meditating in the New Age manner, she asked God to send her to a teacher and the name Ramadya came to her mind. Later when she met a well-known spiritual healer, the woman described a guru that appeared to be what she was looking for. A short time later Clare met a guru at the yoga center whose name was in Ramaya.

After studying New Age theory and yoga for two more years, she enrolled in a four-year program in spiritual healing with one of the foremost leaders of the New Age movement. This program involved working with spiritual guides and angels in order to channel energy for healing. In her class, were a large variety of professional people, such as doctors, lawyers, psychologists, and physicists.

In time, Clare came to see "auras" and see or hear angels and develop powers of prophecy and discernment. The well-known woman that Clare studied with "channeled an entity" to enter her body. This woman claims now to be receiving the Eucharist from the Virgin Mary.

"Channeling" is one of the elements of New Age spirituality. A medium in a trance lets various entities take over his/her body. There is a wide range of these entities; some of them are said to dwell in inner planes that can be reached only by using drugs, special rituals, and altered states of consciousness.

Finally, at a weekend workshop something happened which caused Clare to break with New Age. One of the members of her group was declared to be a war-lock and his romantic partner became psychotic. In fear, others also left the group. Clare reports: "I, myself, became terror-stricken by the events that were unfolding." (6) Meanwhile, the woman in charge of the program changed back and forth from one personality to another.

Unable to sleep for four days, Clare, fearing possession or insanity, went to see a priest. The priest, who was active in deliverance ministry, talked to her and went to make a phone call upstairs. When he came back, he was visibly upset and inquired if she had followed him, which, of course, she had not. When she began to talk to him, he grew very sleepy and she saw that her brother who had accom-panied her to the rectory had fallen asleep. The priest quickly said a blessing and dismissed her.

Upon returning home, she phoned a priest who had helped her family in the past. He prayed for her over the phone and as she hung up, she was slain in the spirit for the first time in her life.

She believes that the real Jesus of Nazareth appeared to her. She writes:

> At that moment, a figure I firmly believe was Jesus Christ came to me, and over a period of what seemed a half-hour put me through a grueling and terri-fying deliverance. This was not the New Age 'christ' of hearts and flowers and angel bells, but the true Jesus Christ who commanded me to renounce the life I had come to lead. There are no words to explain the physical and spiritual

deliverance that took place inside of me. It felt as if the Lord were taking me apart and putting me back together again." (6)

It took Clare five years to be healed of these traumatic experiences. During this time she felt like she was in hell. Her feelings of heat, anguish, and fear were vanquished by a visit to a monastery where the Blessed Mother healed her. She is now aware of God's love and the knowledge that she is God's temple and that she had violated that temple by renouncing her faith and Jesus Christ. She now speaks whenever she can and writes articles to help others who are trapped in New Age. She writes: "Never as before, Christians who have become involved in the many dangerous practices of the New Age, from Reiki, yoga, and meditation, to trance channeling and energy healing, are suffering severe repercussions. Many of them are practicing Marian Catholics, taken in by practices such as Heal Touch International and Reiki, very popular among Catholic medical professionals and church ministry leaders." (6)

She concludes her life story by saying that we need to "pray and intercede for our loved ones and our friends who are unwittingly bringing into our families and congregations the poisons of the New Age which are denial, narcissism, arrogance and spiritual bondage." She points out that "the cancers of abortion, population control, and euthanasia" that we are exporting around the globe are condoned by New Age and seen by them as works of mercy. "Nowadays, I take great joy in sharing this most precious faith to which Our Lord and Lady have restored me. We truly have a treasure whose worth is unknown, a truth that really does set us free and keeps us safe—in the arms of Jesus and Mary" (6).

Others who have found that New Age practice is to be avoided are members of the Society of Jesus who used to promote the Enneagram, a system that is supposed to reveal nine personality types. Fr. Mitch Pacwa, SJ has written an interesting article titled "The Enneagram: Spirituality It is Not." He debunks the New Age claim that the Enneagram is a 2000-year-old System developed by Islamic mystics. All educated people know that Islam did not exist 2000 years ago.

One story goes that the Enneagram was promoted about 1900 by a man named George Ilych Gurdjieff who was half Armenian and half Greek. As a youth he was in a seminary, but left by the age of thirteen to follow the occult. He is said to have discovered the Enneagram among a group of Sufis in Central Asia.

Others like one Don Riso, an ex Jesuit, say that Oscar Ichazo invented the Enneagram. Father Pacwa explains:

In one of Don Riso's books, he said that Oscar Ichazo, a Chilean occultist, is in contact with spirits like Metraton, the chief of the archangels. I [Fr. Pacwa] said wait a minute. Whose side is that Archangel on? I don't think it's St. Michael's.

Oscar Ichazo claims to have the source of all grace on planet earth today. All grace on the earth comes through Ichazo. He is in contact with all the ascended masters and is himself an ascended master. He was given the Enneagram personality types by his spirit, Metraton. Metraton told him to take the Enneagram—just as a drawing without any names on it—and on the Enneagram, place the capital sins." (Pacwa, "The Enneagram)

The Jesuits got involved with the Enneagram and began teaching it at a course at the Jesuit School of Theology. However, Fr. Pacwa now assures us that there is not a single member of the Society of Jesus left who is teaching it. He remarks that the one who gave fifty-two Enneagram seminars a year at the Jesuit retreat center in Cleveland drove it bankrupt. He observes that two Dominicans, a priest and a nun, were working full time with the Enneagram, but it put them out of business also.

The main complaint Fr. Pacwa makes about the use of the Enneagram is that "goofy advice is being given in spiritual direction on the basis of this."

Fr. Pacwa reports reading some books written on the Enneagram by some of its newer advocates. One is a nun in the Philippines, the other a Benedictine from Chicago. The Benedictine nun has written a book on how to use the Enneagram to type people and also another book on spiritual direction. In her book on spiritual direction, she mentions Jesus Christ only once and God seven times. "What is she directing these people towards? asks Fr. Pacwa.[2]

Obviously the New Age is in diametric opposition to our Christian faith. To conclude this chapter we quote what John Paul II has to say speaking of the Gnosticism of the New Age movement:

A separate issue is the return of *ancient gnostic ideas under the guise of the so-called New Age.* We cannot delude ourselves that this will lead toward a renewal of religion. It is only a new way of practicing gnosticism—that attitude of spirit that, in the name of a profound knowledge of God, results in distorting His Word and replacing it with purely human words. Gnosticism never completely abandoned the realm of Christianity. Instead, it has always existed side by side with Christianity, sometimes taking the shape of a philosophical movement, but more often assuming the characteristics of a religion or para-religion in distinct, if not declared, conflict with all that is essentially Christian. (*Crossing the Threshold of Hope* 90)

Be Free to Grow

When we are going on a journey, we decide what we need to take with us and begin packing. The longer the journey the more we will have to do to get ready for it and the more things we will have to pack in our luggage. The greatest journey of life is the spiritual one we make on our way to God. It too requires some planning if we are going to arrive without many detours and hazards. If we are spiritual dwarfs, we will not have the necessary things to travel well and arrive in top form at our destination. We need to grow in the spiritual life.

With many Catholics, Confirmation marks the end of learning about their faith and how to live it. We have seen in the past twenty years a decline in the number of people using the Sacrament of Reconciliation, yet many of us spend years of our lives confessing the same sins, year in and year out. When it comes time to leave this world, some of us will try to take a crash course to get ready for heaven, failing to understand that heaven begins on earth as we accept Jesus Christ as Lord of our lives. We are judged every time we listen to the Word of God, as we accept it or reject it, as we decide our own eternal fate. When we face the Lord in the life to come, we will hear Him confirm the decisions that we ourselves made in this life.

How do we grow in the spiritual life? Basically we grow through discipleship, learning from our Savior Jesus Christ how to pray, how to deal with life, how to defeat sinfulness through His power and grace. As we follow Him, we learn to deny ourselves, carry our cross, and are purified by the trials that come to us. Prayer and the acquisition of virtue go hand in hand. Because the spiritual life is a whole, an increase of one, brings about in us an increase of the other, generally speaking.

At the beginning of our lives, we learn a few vocal prayers that we repeat before we go to bed at night. The prayers we learned are very good, but we need to advance beyond them to praying in our own words. Children should be taught to talk to Jesus when they make their first Holy Communion, which is a good time for them to begin developing mental prayer.

Speaking of the soul's ascent to God, St. Bonaventure writes: "Since happiness is nothing other than the enjoyment of the highest good and since the highest good is above, no one can be made happy unless he rise above himself, not by an ascent of the body, but of the heart" (Bonaventure 59). The saint goes on to explain that we need divine aid to make progress in the spiritual life. "Prayer, then, is the mother and source of the ascent" (60).

Let us see what Holy Scripture has to say about prayer. First, what exactly is prayer? Prayer is described as lifting up the soul to God. David exclaims, "To you, O Lord, have I lifted up my soul" (Ps 24. 1). In Psalm 85, the psalmist begs God for mercy saying, "Have mercy on me, O Lord, for I have cried to thee all the day" (3). So prayer can be described as crying out to God. In the book of Revelation, prayer is compared to a fragrance. "And when he had opened the book, the living creatures, and the four and twenty ancients fell down before the Lamb, having every one of them harps, and golden vials full of odors, which are the prayers of the saints" (5: 8) In our churches the pungent fragrance of incense rises up around the altar like prayer.

Prayer can also be described as coming to the throne of grace as in, "Let us go therefore with confidence to the throne of grace that we may obtain mercy and find grace in seasonable aid" (Heb 4: 16). The author of the book of Hebrews also refers to prayer as a "sacrifice of praise" and "the fruit of lips confessing His name" (13: 15). And finally Holy Scripture refers to prayer as drawing near to God. "Draw nigh to God, and He will draw nigh to you" (Jas 4: 8).

There are various kinds of prayer. However the most important element of prayer is the relationship we have with God to whom we should lovingly communicate as to our father, for He authentically *is* our Father. Consider how Abraham, the chosen one of God, confides in God as one confides in a friend, trusting God as a child trusts his father. We need to remember that we have not "received the spirit of bondage again in fear," but we have received the spirit of adoption of sons, whereby we cry: Abba (Father)" (Rom 8: 15).

We must approach God with loving hearts free from fear, remembering that Jesus has a plan for salvation, not a plan for condemnation. We know that hell exists, but God loves us as a father loves his little child. We must talk to him with confidence and open hearts. He knows what we need, before we ask Him. He wants what is good for us even more than we do. We must remember that if human fathers know how to give good gifts to their children, God knows even better how to care for us. If we ask for bread, he will not give us snakes or scorpions.

Our relationship with the Heavenly Father must be in the power of the Holy Spirit, who helps us to know what we should pray for. As St. Paul says, "Likewise the Spirit also helps our infirmity. For we know not what we should pray for as we ought; but the Spirit himself asks for us with unspeakable groanings" (Ro 8: 26). If we are open in our relationship with God, the Holy Spirit tells us what to ask for and what words to use in praying. God is a person and desires to have a personal relationship with each of us. We come to God in prayer, because the Holy Spirit draws us.

We need to listen to the Spirit and conform to what He tells us. How simple it is to conform to what the Spirit puts in our hearts, minds, and mouths, teaching us to pray according to the will of God. The elemental principal of all prayer is conforming to the will of God. This is very important to remember, for we are to yield to the desires and wishes of God. God will mold our hearts and teach us what is really important. Submitting to the will of God means realizing that He has a perfect plan for our lives, for our salvation, and for our glorification.

When we come into the presence of God, Holy Scripture gives us many examples of how we should act. In a very dramatic scene, the prophet Isaiah experienced the necessity of confessing his sinfulness when he had a vision of the glory of God. In the year that King Uzziah, the tenth king of Judah, died, 731 BC, Isaiah saw the Lord sitting upon a high throne with his train filling the temple. Above the throne, he beheld the six-winged seraphim who were calling out to each other: "Holy, holy, holy, the Lord God of hosts, all the earth is full of His glory" (Is 6: 3). So overwhelming was their hymn of praise that even the door lintels trembled at the sound of it. Smoke filled the place. Awestricken Isaiah exclaims: "Woe is me, because I have held my peace; because I am a man of unclean lips, and I dwell in the midst of a people that has unclean lips, and I have seen with my eyes the King, the Lord of hosts" (Is 6: 5). He is filled with self-reproach because he remained silent while the angels praise God incessantly. Also no doubt he recalled the ancient belief that no man could see God and live.

One of the seraphim flew to Isaiah with tongs containing a burning coal that he had taken off the altar. Touching Isaiah's lips with the burning coal, the seraph proclaimed: "Behold this has touched your lips, and your iniquities shall be taken away, and your sin shall be cleansed" (6: 7).

Cleansed of his sins, Isaiah now hears the voice of the Lord asking, "Whom shall I send? And who shall go for us?" (6: 8).

"Here I am; send me," replied Isaiah (6:9).

Then the Lord communicated the message He wished Isaiah to take to the children of Israel.

The prophet Daniel also confessed his sins, when he entered the presence of the Lord and begged Him to spare His people who had sinned greatly and had been punished by being taken captive into Babylon, modern Iraq. Daniel's prayer is very powerful and an example of how to pray effectively. The date of the prayer is 538 B.C., one year before Cyrus permitted the Jews to return from exile. Daniel himself tells about his prayer:

> And I set my face to the Lord my God, to pray and make supplication with fasting, and sackcloth, and ashes." (Dan 9: 3) And I prayed to the Lord my God, and I made my confession, and said: I beseech You, O Lord God, great and terrible, who keeps the covenant, and mercy to them that love You, and keep Your commandments. (9: 4)

> We have sinned, we have committed iniquity, we have done wickedly, and have revolted, and we have gone aside your commandments, and your judgments. (9:5)

> We have not hearkened to your servants the prophets that have spoken in your name to our kings, to our princes, to our fathers, and to all the people of the land.

> To you, O Lord, justice, but to us confusion of face, as at this day to the men of Judah, and to the inhabitants of Jerusalem, and to all Israel to them that are near, and to them that are far off in all the countries whither you have driven them, for their iniquities by which they have sinned against you.

> O Lord, to us belongs confusion of face, to our princes, and to our fathers that have sinned. But to You, the Lord our God, mercy and forgiveness, for we have departed from You and we have not hearkened to the voice of the Lord our God, to walk in His law, which He set before us by His servants the prophets. And all Israel have transgressed Your law, and have turned away from hearing Your voice, and the malediction, and the curse, which is written in the book of Moses the servant of God, is fallen upon us, because we have sinned against Him. And He has confirmed His words, which He spoke against us, and against our princes that judged us, that He would bring in upon us a great evil, such as never was under all the heaven, according to that which has been done in Jerusalem. As it is written in the Law of Moses, all this evil is come upon us, and we entreated not Your face, O Lord our God, that we might turn from our iniquities, and think on Your truth.

> And the Lord has watched upon the evil, and hath brought it upon us, the Lord our God is just in all His works, which He has done: for we have not hearkened to His voice.

> And now, O Lord our God, who has brought forth Your people out of the land of Egypt with a strong hand, and has made You a name as at this day, we have sinned, we have committed iniquity, O Lord, against all Your justice: let Your wrath and Your indignation be turned away, I beseech You, from Your

city Jerusalem, and from Your holy mountain. For by reason of our sins, and the iniquities of our fathers, Jerusalem, and Your people are a reproach to all that are round about us. Now therefore, O our God, hear the supplication of Your servant, and his prayers: and show Your face upon Your sanctuary, which is desolate, for Your own sake.

Incline, O my God, Your ear and hear; open Your eyes, and see our desolation, and the city upon which Your name is called, for it is not for our justifications that we present our prayers before Your face, but for the multitude of Your tender mercies.

O Lord, hear. O Lord, be appeased, hearken, and do; delay not for Your own sake, O my God, because Your name is invocated upon Your city, and upon Your people. (Dan 9: 19)

Moved by the earnestness of his confession and his petition for help, God sent an angel to Daniel. Gabriel flew to him and touched him at the time of the evening sacrifice and spoke to him, "O Daniel, I am now come forth to teach you, and that you might understand" (Dan 9: 20).

Just as Isaiah and Daniel confess their sinfulness and the iniquity of their people, we too must remove sin from our lives if we want God to answer our prayer. Isaiah explains this clearly: "Your iniquities have divided between you and your God, and your sins have hid His face from you that He should not hear. For your hands are defiled with blood, and your fingers with iniquity; your lips have spoken lies, and your tongue utters iniquity" (Is 59: 2–3).

Furthermore, we have to forgive others if we want God to forgive us. Our Lord, Himself, tells us this: "For if you will forgive men their offences, your heavenly Father will forgive you also your offences. But if you will not forgive men, neither will your Father forgive you your offences" (Mt 6: 14–15). St. John the Evangelist tells us that if we confess our sins, God will forgive us. However, "if we say that we have not sinned, we make Him a liar, and His word is not in us" (1 Jn 1: 10).

Let us now turn to considering the various types of prayer, beginning with adoration, praise, and thanksgiving—ways of prayer that are most pleasing to the Triune God. The psalmist declares: "The heavens shall confess Your wonders, O Lord, and Your truth in the church of the saints. O Lord God of hosts, who is like to You? You are mighty, O Lord, and Your truth is round about you" (88: 6–7). "Sing to the Lord a new canticle; let His praise be in the church of the saints" (149: 1).

The psalms are filled with adoration and praise. "Let them give praise to Your great name, for it is terrible and holy" (98:3). "Exalt the Lord our God, and adore His footstool, for it is holy" (Ps 98: 5).

Let us learn praise and adoration from the angels. At the birth of Christ they sang as Luke reports: "And suddenly there was with the angel a multitude of the heavenly army, praising God, and saying: "Glory to God in the highest; and on earth peace to men of good will" (Lk 2: 13–14). The author of the book of Revelation describes the praise and adoration of the angels and the ancient ones.

> And the four living creatures had each of them six wings, and round about and within, they are full of eyes. And they rested not day and night, saying: "Holy, holy, holy, Lord God Almighty, who was, and who is, and who is to come."

> And when those living creatures gave glory, and honor, and benediction to Him that sits on the throne, who lives forever and ever, the four and twenty ancients fell down before Him that sits on the throne, and adored Him that lives for ever and ever, and cast their crowns before the throne, saying: "You are worthy, O Lord our God, to receive glory, and honor, and power: because You have created all things; and for Your will they were, and have been created." (Rev 4: 5–22)

In addition to praising God and adoring Him without ceasing for His great glory, we must also thank Him. "Pray without ceasing. In all things give thanks; for this is the will of God in Christ Jesus concerning you all" (1 Th 5: 17–18). St. Paul exhorts us to be faithful in giving thanks and in praying continually. "Be nothing solicitous; but in every thing, by prayer and supplication, with thanksgiving, let your petitions be made known to God" (Php 4:6). And when we give thanks for everything we have, we are to do it in the name of our Lord, "Giving thanks always for all things, in the name of our Lord Jesus Christ, to God and the Father" (Eph 5: 20).

We must be cognizant of the fact that ingratitude is sin. In the gospel the story of the ten lepers who were healed shows us the sin of ingratitude at work in the hearts of men. Only one of the ten who were healed came back to Jesus, fell on his face before His feet and glorified God" (Lk 17: 15.) He was a Samaritan, not one of God's chosen people who should know their obligation to give God praise and thanksgiving. Jesus addressed him: "Were not ten made clean? Where are the nine? There is no one found to return and give glory to God, but this stranger" (Lk 17: 16–18).

In the book of Romans, St. Paul also speaks of what happens to those who do not glorify God and give Him thanks and praise.

> For the invisible things of Him, from the creation of the world, are clearly seen, being understood by the things that are made; His eternal power also, and divinity, so that they are inexcusable. Because that, when they knew God, they have not glorified him as God, or given thanks; but became vain in their thoughts, and their foolish heart was darkened. For professing themselves to be wise, they became fools. And they changed the glory of the incorruptible God into the likeness of the image of a corruptible man, and of birds, and of four-footed beasts, and of creeping things. Wherefore God gave them up to the desires of their heart, unto uncleanness, to dishonor their own bodies among themselves. Who changed the truth of God into a lie, and worshipped and served the creature rather than the Creator, who is blessed forever. Amen. (Rom 1: 20–25)

Ingratitude is a sin that we as children of God must avoid, if we want to please Him and grow in the spiritual life.

God seems to enjoy the prayer of petition in which we ask Him for our needs and the needs of others. Asking is an act of humility, and as we present our needs to Him we recognize His power above us. When we pray for our daily needs, we should pray for wisdom and health, and to resist temptation.

St. Paul tells us that we are not to worry about anything, "but in every thing, by prayer and supplication, with thanksgiving, let your petitions be made known to God" (Php 4: 6). The Apostle James encourages us to pray for wisdom: "if any of you want wisdom, let him ask of God, who gives to all men abundantly, and upbraids not; and it shall be given him" (Jas 1: 5). We are to ask in faith without wavering, because if we waver we are like an ocean wave that is blown hither and yon by the wind and we shall receive nothing from God. (Jas 1: 7).

Following the example of St. Paul, we may pray for our problems and infirmities. He tells us this:

> And lest the greatness of the revelations should exalt me, there was given me a sting of my flesh, an angel of Satan, to buffet me, for which thing thrice I besought the Lord, that it might depart from me. And he said to me: "My grace is sufficient for thee; for power is made perfect in infirmity." Gladly therefore will I glory in my infirmities, that the power of Christ may dwell in me." (2 Cor 12: 7)

If God chooses not to answer our prayer in the way we had hope, we must like Paul, glory in our infirmities, realizing that God knows what is best for us.

It is important to understand that we do not pray alone, but the Lord Jesus is our great High Priest who lives to make intercession for us. "Whereby He is able also to save forever them that come to God by Him; always living to make inter-cession for us" (Heb 7: 25). He is our holy, innocent, undefiled High Priest who offered Himself up in sacrifice for us on Calvary. He has entered "heaven itself, that he may appear now in the presence of God for us" (Heb 9: 24).

The Holy Spirit also helps us by interceding for us. As St. Paul states: "Like-wise the Spirit also helps our infirmity. For we know not what we should pray for, as we ought; but the Spirit himself asks for us with unspeakable groanings. And He that searches the hearts, knows what the Spirit desires, because He asks for the saints according to God" (Rom 8: 26–27).

When the apostles asked the Lord to teach them to pray, He gave them the prayer we refer to as the Lord's Prayer or the Our Father. Ever since the earliest centuries of the Church, people have written explanations of this prayer. One of the earliest writers was Quintus Septimus Florens Tertullianus, better known simply as Tertullian, who was born about 150 or 160 in Carthage as the son of a centurion in the proconsular service. It appears that he was an advocate in the courts of law. A well-educated man who knew both Latin and Greek, he was a pagan until about 197 when he ardently converted to Christianity. Not long after his conversion he was ordained a priest about the year 200 for the church in Carthage in Africa. Unfortunately, he did not stay loyal to the teaching magiste-rium of the Church and sometime after the year 206, he joined the Montanists, a sect founded by a prophet, Montanus, and two prophetesses, Maximilla and Prisca, sometimes called Priscilla, all who claimed to be possessed by God.

He parted company with the Montanists and founded a sect of his own, the Tertullianists, who were finally reconciled to the Church by St. Augustine. He wrote an attack on a bishop, probably Pope Callistus, sometime after 218. Because he was especially displeased with the Catholic Church since it approved of second marriages, and he did not, he began vehement attacks. The Church has always permitted widows and widowers second marriages. According to St. Jer-ome, Tertullian lived to extreme old age.

Tertullian's treatise on the Lord's Prayer does not contain any elements of the Montanists' doctrines. An excellent writer, Tertullian has provided us with an interesting study of prayer in the early centuries of the Catholic Church, as the Church was already referred to in those early days.

In the first chapter, Tertullian makes a very good observation about the Lord's Prayer, by saying that "in the Prayer is comprised an epitome of the whole gos-pel." Commenting on the first clause of the prayer, "Our Father who art in heaven," he remarks: "Happy they who recognize their Father!" When we pray that the Father's name be hallowed, according to Tertullian, we are praying that

God's name "be hallowed in us who are in Him, as well as in all others for whom the grace of God is still waiting." In praying "Thy will be done in the heavens and on earth" we are asking Him "to supply us with the substance of His will" and the ability to carry it out both in heaven and on earth, "because the sum of His will is the salvation of them whom He has adopted." When we pray "Thy kingdom come" we are praying for the end of the age. "Our wish is, that our reign be hastened [the life of the world to come], not our servitude [life in this world] protracted. In praying for our daily bread, we may understand our daily bread in a spiritual way:

> For Christ is our Bread; because Christ is Life, and bread is life. "I am," says He, "the bread of Life, and a little above [in the Scripture passage], "The Bread is the Word of the living God, who came down from the heavens." Then we find, too, that His Body is reckoned in bread: "This is my Body." And so, in petitioning for "daily bread," we ask for perpetuity in Christ, and indivisibility from His body. (VI)

In asking the Lord to forgive us our debts, we are making a full confession of our guilt. To Tertullian, the phrase "Lead us not into temptation" signifies that we are asking God to keep us safe from the evil one. In conclusion, he especially recommends the Lord's Prayer to all believers, because "God alone could teach how He wished Himself prayed to" (IX).

Interestingly St. Cyprian, bishop and martyr, also of Carthage wrote a treatise on the Lord's Prayer, which resembles Tertullian's. We know virtually nothing of this author's birth and early years. He was probably well into the middle years of his life when he became a Christian, during the Easter Vigil, April 18, 246.

On August 30, 257 St. Thaschus Cæcilius Cyprianus was brought before the Proconsul Paternus; the interrogation he endured is contained in the "Acta proconsularia" of his martyrdom. In September, he was sent into exile in Curubis, accompanied by one Pontius. The first night he was there he dreamed that he had been sentenced to die. He wrote to nine other bishops in Numidia who were having more difficulties than he, being forced to work in the mines, without sufficient food and clothing. Since he was still a wealthy man, he was able to give them aid.

In August, 258, Cyprian learned that the Holy Father, Pope Sixtus, had been martyred in the catacombs. Galerius Maximus who succeeded Paternus had St. Cyprian returned to Carthage where he was arrested in his own gardens. On the morning of the fourteenth, Cyprian was tried at the villa of one Sextus. When he refused to sacrifice to the pagan gods, he told them there was no room for thinking about any consequences that might result. When the proconsul read his condemnation, the large crowd assembled there wanted to be beheaded with him. The authorities took him to a hollow encircled with trees. After taking off his cloak and vestments, he knelt down and prayed in his linen tunic waiting for the executioner. He ordered that the executioner be paid twenty-five pieces gold. With the help of a priest and a deacon, he bandaged his eyes, while the faithful put cloths and handkerchiefs in front of him to catch his blood. His head was severed from his body. For the rest of the day, his body was displayed for the pagans to see. That night, the Christian people processing with candles and torches bore his body to the cemetery Macrobius Candidianus in the suburb of Mapalia. He was the first Bishop of Carthage to obtain the crown of martyrdom.

In his treatise on the Lord's Prayer, St. Cyprian asks "What can be a more spiritual prayer than that which was given to us by Christ, by whom also the Holy Spirit was given to us?" (2). He then goes on to exhort his people to pray as Jesus has taught us, commenting on how much more effectively we receive what we ask in Christ's name when we ask using his own prayer.

Where should we pray? St. Cyprian reminds us that the Lord has told us to pray in secret, quietly remembering, "God is the hearer, not of the voice, but of the heart" (4). Above all we are not to pray for ourselves alone. We do not pray "My Father," but rather "Our Father." "Our prayer is public and common, and when we pray, we pray not for one, but for the whole people, because we the whole people are one" (8). Pointing to the prayer of the apostles with Mary, the Mother of Jesus, in the upper room he notes: "They continued with one accord in prayer, declaring both by the urgency and by the agreement of their praying that God, 'who makes men to dwell of one mind in a house,' only admits into the divine and eternal home those among whom prayer is unanimous" (8).

Remarking on all that is contained in The Lord's Prayer, he states: "How many and how great, briefly collected in the words, but spiritually abundant in virtue, so that there is absolutely nothing passed over that is nor comprehended in our prayers and petitions, as in a compendium of heavenly doctrine" (9).

To emphasize the wonders of being children of the Heavenly Father, Cyprian comments:

> We ought then when we call God Father, we ought to act as God's children; so that in the measure in which we find pleasure in considering God as a Father, He might also be able to find pleasure in us. Let us converse as temples of God, that it may be plain that God dwells in us. (11)

When we pray, "Hallowed be Thy name," we are asking that His name be hallowed in us—that we will be sanctified. The petition "Thy kingdom come" asks that "the kingdom of God may be set forth to us, even as we also ask that His name may be sanctified in us.

> We pray that our kingdom, which has been promised us by God, may come, which was acquired by the blood and passion of Christ; that we who first are His subjects in the world, may hereafter reign with Christ when He reigns, as He Himself promises and says, "Come ye blessed of my Father, receive the kingdom which has been prepared for you from the beginning of the world." (13)

Next, we pray that we may do as God wills and that includes His giving us His strength and grace, so that we will be able to do it. When we ask that the will of God be done both in heaven and on earth, we are asking that it be done in us, for we are both earth, body, and heaven, spirit.

"Give us this day our daily bread" is a prayer for the Eucharist. "For Christ is the bread of life; and this bread does not belong to all men, but it is ours" (18). "And therefore we ask that our bread—that is Christ—may be given to us daily, that we who abide and live in Christ may not depart from His sanctification and body" (18).

Since we daily ask God to forgive us our sins, we know that we sin daily. If we want God to forgive us our sins, we must forgive those who have hurt us in any way. When we pray, "Lead us not into temptation," we are acknowledging our weakness and infirmity and that we need God's help to live good lives. With the final phrase, "Deliver us from evil," we obtain God's help in overcoming all evil that may be directed at us.

Resembling the treatises of Cyprian and Tertullian, St. Augustine preached a number of sermons on the Lord's Prayer. We will consider one of them that he composed for the catechumens who were preparing to receive baptism, confirmation, and the Holy Eucharist.

St Augustine was born November 13, 354 in Tagaste near the ancient Numidian city of Hippo-Regius in what is today Algeria. Although his father Patricius was a pagan when Augustine was born, he became a Christian because of the intercession of his wife Monica and was baptized and died a holy death about 371. Augustine, still not baptized, went to Carthage as a student about the year 370. Soon he met a woman who bore him a son in 372. The following year he became interested in the practices of the heretical Manicheans. Apparently to escape from his mother's influence, Augustine went to Rome in 383 where he opened a school of rhetoric. He later obtained a position as a professor in Milan where he encountered St. Ambrose who finally brought him into the Catholic Church. Augustine related the full account of his conversion in his *Confessions*, a book that we highly recommend. St. Ambrose in Milan baptized him during the Easter season in 387. In 388 he returned to Tagaste. Although he had not planned to become a priest, one day when he was praying in a church in Hippo, a throng of people spotted him, and cheering begged Bishop Valerius to ordain Augustine to the priesthood. The ordination took place in 391. When he was forty-two years old, aging Bishop Valerius made Augustine a coadjutor bishop. He occupied the See of Hippo for thirty-four years. After a long and fruitful life in the service of the Church, he died 28 August, 430, at the age of seventy-six.

At the beginning of his sermon VI to those seeking admittance into the Church, he cautions them that there are two things we should beware of in prayer. The first is that we should not ask for the wrong things and, second, we should not ask from the forces of evil. With a stern warning he advises that if we pray for evil on our enemies, our prayer will be turned into sin (2). One should not pray with "much speaking;" what one needs to pray is "piety, not wordiness" (4). After explaining that the Lord knows what we need, before we ask him, he insists that He still wants us to pray.

> It is His will that you should pray, that He may give to you longings, that His gifts may not be lightly esteemed; seeing He has Himself formed this longing desire in us. The words therefore that our Lord Jesus Christ has taught us in His prayer are the rule and standard of our desires. You may not ask for anything but what is written there." (4)

Here we note that Augustine teaches that when we desire something it is quite possible that the Lord has put the desire in our hearts, because he wants to give it to us. Although, he believes that we should not request things of God that are not included in the Lord's Prayer, he sees this prayer as encompassing all our needs. When we pray "hallowed be thy Name," Augustine agrees with Cyprian that what we are praying for is our sanctification. When we pray "Thy kingdom come," we are praying God's kingdom may be found in us. "For come it certainly will; but what will it profit you, if it shall find you at the left hand." In this part of the prayer, we are praying that we may live well and not resist the will of God. Also following Cyprian's thought about "in heaven and in earth," Augustine says that the mind is heaven—Cyprian said the spirit—and the flesh is earth and we are praying for them to be in harmony. "We wish for perfection, when we pray for this," the saint explains (8). In praying "Give us this day our daily bread," we become beggars. And just what is this bread we are begging God to give us? All the things we really need are included in this petition. However, first and foremost for the Word of God, which is dealt out to us day by day. Our bread is daily bread; and by it live not our bodies, but our souls. It is necessary for us who are even now laborers in the vineyard—it is our food, not our hire. Our hire after labor is called eternal life" (10).

We now pray that we may live in such a manner that we will never be separated from the Holy Altar by our sins. Since the people to whom he is addressing the homily are about to receive baptism, St. Augustine tells them that they will come up from the baptismal font sinless. After baptism and their reception into the Church, he insists that they will need a daily cleansing from sin. "Alms and prayers purge away sins; only let not such sins be committed, for which we must necessarily be separated from our daily Bread; we avoid all such debts for which a severe and certain condemnation is due" (12). Finally, we must forgive all who have sinned against us, if we want the Lord to forgive us. Moreover, Augustine comments that if we do not love our enemies, we should not pray for God to forgive us as we forgive others.

These thoughts from the early Church Fathers on the Lord's Prayer should help to make our prayer life richer. A good way to pray the Our Father is very slowly word by word, lingering on each word until we have extracted from it everything we can. One could spend fifteen minutes and even longer just contemplating what it means to call God "Father." By praying in this way the Holy Spirit can lift us up to the higher realms of prayer and fill us with His presence. If the Spirit causes us to linger for a long time in certain places of the prayer, we should let Him and go with Him wherever He leads us. He can infuse us with beautiful graces of prayer that will set our souls on fire with the love of God. He can set us free to worship the Father in spirit and in truth.

"Holy Spirit, fire of Divine Love, we ask you to guide us in prayer so that our prayer will be pleasing incense rising up to heaven. Lead us to Jesus that we may contemplate His beauty and become more like Him day by day.

"Lord Jesus, lift us up to the Father, that we may love Him with Your love.

"Holy Trinity, Most High God, we adore you present in the High Heavens and in the souls of the just. Amen."

Free from Death

One of the most beautiful and powerful confessions of faith in the resurrection is found in the oldest book of the Bible when Job exclaims: "I know that my Redeemer lives, and in the last day I shall rise out of the earth. And I shall be clothed again with my skin, and in my flesh I will see my God, whom I myself shall see, and my eyes shall behold, and not another; this my hope is laid up in my bosom" (Job 19: 25–27). We can imagine the joy of Job when He saw Jesus who after the crucifixion went to Sheol or Hades, as the Greeks called it, bringing His redemption to free the holy souls that had gone there before Him. Although the author is not specified, an ancient homily for Holy Saturday quoted in the *Catechism of the Catholic Church* describes this event of Christ going to the netherworld:

> Today a great silence reigns on earth, a great silence and a great stillness. A great silence because the King is asleep. The earth trembled and is still because God has fallen sleep in the flesh and He has raised up all who have slept ever since the world began. He has gone to search for Adam, our first father, as for a lost sheep. Greatly desiring to visit those who live in darkness and in the shadow of death, He has gone to free from sorrow Adam in his bonds and Eve, captive with him—He who is both their God and the son of Eve. "I am your God, who for your sake have become your son… I order you, O sleeper, to awake. I did not create you to be a prisoner in hell. Rise from the dead, for I am the life of the dead. (165)

Christ has conquered death! In His apocalyptic vision in the book of Revelation, St. John quotes Christ as saying: "Fear not. I am the First and the Last, and alive, and was dead, and behold I am living forever and ever, and have the keys of death and of hell" (Rev 1: 17–18).

Death is the last enemy to be conquered (1Co 15:26). Just as in Adam all men die, all who are in Christ never die. We who are in Christ are already in eternal life. The Scripture says that "this is eternal life—that they may know You, the only true God, and Jesus Christ, whom You have sent" (Jn 17: 3). As John Paul II says in *Evangelium Vitae*, "To know God and his Son is to accept the mystery of loving communion of the Father, the Son, and the Holy Spirit into one's own life, which even now is open to eternal life because it shares in the life of God" (Ch 2, 37).

If we know God and Jesus, His Son, we have eternal life now and we shall never die. We will walk through the valley of the shadow of death, but a shadow cannot hurt us, for Christ has freed us from death. Jesus is Life and His life is our light and our salvation. God sent Him to us so that if we believe in Him we shall not die. He did not send His son to condemn us, but to give us life that never ends. Not only is Jesus Life, He is also Truth, and the Way to God, heaven, and eternal life. Consider the following:

A young man approached Jesus and asked him:

"Good master, what good shall I do that I may have life everlasting?

"If you will enter into life, keep the commandments," Jesus replied.

"Which?"

"You shall do no murder. You shall not commit adultery. You shall not steal. You shall not bear false witness. Honor your father and your mother. And you shall love thy neighbor as thyself."

"All these I have kept from my youth, what is yet wanting to me?"

"If you will be perfect, go sell what you have, and give to the poor, and you shall have treasure in heaven, and come follow me."

Obviously Jesus is asking the young man to practice charity by giving to the poor. Sadly the young man went away from Jesus, because he had great possessions and did not want to part with them as a condition for following Christ. When the man was gone Jesus said to his disciples:

"It is easier for a camel to pass through the eye of a needle, than for a rich man to enter into the kingdom of heaven" (Mt 19: 16–24).

Visiting Jerusalem, we learned that the "eye of the needle" is the small door that has been made in the large gates of the city so that people can pass through, but camels cannot. However, it is not impossible for a camel to pass through "the eye of the needle," but in order to do so, it has to get down on its knees, getting rid of what it is carrying. And so the rich must do if they want to enter everlasting life.

We know that the Twelve Apostles gave up everything to follow Jesus, but they were a special group. It was not required of others to dispose of all their property. We know that John Mark's mother Mary had a house in Jerusalem (Acts 12: 12) and also Philip the Evangelist had a house in Caesarea. The Apostle Peter told Ananias and Saphira that they were not required to sell their property or give the Church the money, if they did (Acts 4: 4). Apparently the Lord was calling this young man to special service, just as many are called today to the religious life and the giving up of their possessions.

Commenting on this encounter of the rich young man with Jesus, Pope John Paul II say that the question the young man poses about what he has to do to gain eternal life is a question that is in the heart of every individual and it is a question that only Christ can answer. Furthermore, Christ is present in His Church in all ages ready to answer the question for those who ask it. (*Evan Vitae* 25)

We notice in this exchange between Jesus and the rich young man that the Lord puts emphasis on keeping the commandments of God if we want to have everlasting life. Elsewhere Jesus said: "If any one loves me, he will keep my word, and my Father will love him, and we will come to him, and will make our abode with him" (Jn 14: 23). Repeatedly Jesus spoke of coming to be with his followers after He ascended to His Father.

> I will not leave you orphans. I will come to you. Yet a little while: and the world sees me no more. But you see me, because I live, and you shall live. In that day you shall know, that I am in my Father, and you in Me, and I in you. He that has My commandments, and keeps them; he it is that loves Me. And he that loves me shall be loved of My Father: and I will love him, and will manifest Myself to him. (Jn 14: 18–21)

For two millennia Jesus has been manifesting Himself to those that love Him. The lives of the saints are full of accounts telling of their encounters with our Divine Lord. However, the Lord has provided a way for all of us, his followers, to approach Him and have His life—eternal life—within our souls and bodies. While preaching in the synagogue at Capharnaum, He revealed that He is the Living Bread that comes down from heaven. He tells us: "If any man eat of this bread, he shall live for ever, and the bread that I will give, is my flesh, for the life of the world" (Jn 6: 52).

When the people who first heard Jesus proclaim the giving of Himself to be eaten, they were perplexed and thought He was saying something they could not accept. Many of them ceased following him because of this. We notice that He makes no attempt to dissuade them. Instead He reiterates:

> Amen, amen, I say unto you. Except you eat the flesh of the Son of man, and drink His blood, you shall not have life in you. He that eats My flesh and drinks My blood has everlasting life and I will raise him up in the last day. For My flesh is meat indeed and My blood is drink indeed. He that eats My flesh

and drinks My blood abides in Me and I in him. As the Living Father has sent Me, and I live by the Father, so he that eats Me, the same shall live by Me. This is the bread that came down from heaven. Not as your fathers did eat manna, and are all dead. He that eats this bread shall live for ever." (Jn 6: 54–59)

This is the faith of the Church and has been ever since the death, resurrection, and ascension of Jesus—when a priest takes bread and blesses it saying, "This is my body" and takes the cup of wine and blesses it saying, "This is my blood," the bread and the wine are transubstantiated into the Body and Blood, Soul and Divinity of Jesus Christ. They still look like bread and wine, but no longer are. They still have the form of bread and wine, but in substance they are the Body and Blood of Christ. When we partake of His Body and Blood in the Eucharist, we receive Life—our eternal life. We shall never taste death. Christ has defeated death and taken away its sting. It no longer has dominion over us because Jesus rose from the dead nevermore to die.

Our Christian faith is based on the historical fact of Christ's resurrection from the tomb on Easter. After He rose from the dead, Jesus was seen by Peter and then by the rest of the apostles. "Then," St Paul tells us, "he was seen by more than five hundred brethren at once of whom many remain until the present and some are fallen asleep. After that He was seen by James, then by all the apostles and last of all, He was seen also by me, as by one born out of due time" (1 Cor 15: 6–8).

At the time Paul wrote this in his first letter to the Corinthians, there were people who were living at the time of the resurrection who could have refuted his statements, if they had not been accurate and true. However, the word of the apostle should be enough to convince anyone that He was speaking the truth, especially since he died for his belief in the resurrected Lord.

Every one of the apostles was a witness to the resurrection of Jesus. For this reason, the bishops in the Church today should lead the entire Church to witness to the resurrection. Because of the apostolic succession that has been meticulously preserved down through the centuries by the laying on of hands when already consecrated bishops consecrate new bishops, the bishops witness in a special way to the resurrection. The Church, the Body of Christ, one billion forty million strong is a sure witness to the resurrection of Jesus. Therefore we are confident that we too shall rise from the grave to live with Christ. "In a moment, in the twinkling of an eye, at the last trumpet, for the trumpet shall sound, and the dead shall rise again incorruptible, and we shall be changed" (1Co 15: 52). Our mortal bodies will put on immortality and death will be swallowed up in victory (1 Cor 15: 4).

Commenting on our eternal life, John Paul II remarks:

> Here the Christian truth about life becomes most sublime. The dignity of this life is linked not only to its beginning, to the fact that it comes from God, but also to its final end, to its destiny of fellowship with God in knowledge and love of him. In the light of this truth, Saint Irenaeus qualifies and completes praise of man: "the glory of God" is indeed, "man, living man," but "the life of man consists in the vision of God." (*Evan vitae* II, 38)

With grateful hearts we adore the Blessed and Immortal Trinity that offers to share life with us. Thank God who through Jesus Christ gives us the victory over death, sin, and the grave. We are comforted and consoled by the words of Jesus as we live in this word, longing for heaven:

> I am the good shepherd. The good shepherd gives His life for His sheep. And I give them life everlasting and they shall not perish for ever, and no man shall pluck them out of My hand. That which My Father has given Me, is greater than all, and no one can snatch them out of the hand of My Father. I am the resurrection and the life. He that believes in Me, although he be dead, shall live, and every one that lives and believes in Me, shall not die forever. Do you believe this? For I have not spoken of Myself, but the Father who sent Me, He gave me commandment what I should say, and what I should speak, even as the Father said unto Me, so do I speak. (Jn 10: 11, 28, 29; 11: 25,26, 49, 50)

"Dear Lord Jesus, We do believe you. You truly have the words of eternal life. We rejoice knowing that we are in the Father's hand and no one can snatch us out of it. We welcome Your presence into our hearts and souls, receiving Your Body and Blood with deepest gratitude. Holy Spirit, we ask you to guide us on the way to the Father. Heavenly Father we look forward to coming to live with You when this life is over. Holy Trinity we welcome You to come make your abode in us. Fill us with Your presence and bring us safely through the valley of the shadow of death to you in glory. Amen."

Be Free to Live—Forever!

Just what is the freedom Christ gives us? It is life. Freedom is life; slavery is death. Freedom is not license, which is an abuse of freedom. Rather freedom is liberty to live free from slavery, repression, or incarceration and to be governed by consent illuminated by the grace of God. We are made in the image of God, and it us our innermost desire to search for what is good. If we choose to do evil to those we love or ourselves, it is because we mistakenly think that what we are choosing is something good, failing to understand and will true goodness. Specifically, when the Holy Spirits fills our hearts, He guides and directs us so that we are no longer slaves to our passions and desires. He liberates us from sin, which is bondage. Our Lord tells us that whoever commits sin is the servant of sin (Jn 8: 34).

Since we cannot foresee the consequences of our actions with certitude, in this present life we can sin by choosing to do something that appears to be good, but in reality is not. Pope Leo XIII, elected pope 20 February, 1878 and died 20 July, 1903, in his encyclical *Libertas* expounds on this:

> For, as the possibility of error, and actual error, are defects of the mind and attest its imperfection, so the pursuit of what has a false appearance of good, though a proof of our freedom, just as disease is a proof of our vitality, implies a defect in human liberty. The will also, simply because of its dependence on the reason no sooner desires anything contrary thereto than it abuses its freedom of choice and corrupts its very essence. Thus it is that the infinitely perfect God, although supremely free, because of the supremacy of His intellect and of His essential goodness, nevertheless cannot choose evil; neither can the angels and saints, who enjoy the beatific vision. (6)

Similarly, when we are in Christ and filled with the Holy Spirit, we have no desire to go against His teaching. If we love God, we can do what we wish. However we will not wish to do anything that displeases Him and the power of the indwelling Spirit of God enables us to choose life and freedom and reject death and slavery. When our hearts are filled with the love of God we will love God with all our hearts with His own indwelling love and we will love our neighbor as ourselves. As Jesus said, we are to love the Lord our God with our whole hearts, souls, and minds; this is the first and greatest commandment. The second is we shall love our neighbors as ourselves. "On these two commandments depend the whole law and the prophets" (Mt 22: 40). When He sets us free, it is so that we might serve the people of God. In the words of St. Paul, "while we have time, let us work good to all men, but especially to those who are of the household of the faith" (Gal 6: 10).

We all have a very powerful innate desire to live, not just for a few years but forever. It is a desire the Lord has placed in all of us. He also tells us that we are already in eternal life if we know the Heavenly Father and Jesus Christ whom He has sent (John 17: 3). However, as long as we are in the present life in this world, we will not be totally free. "For a just man shall fall seven times and shall rise again: but the wicked shall fall down into evil" (Pr 24: 16). When we finally attain to the state of the blessed in heaven, we will be incapable of making the mistake of choosing sin anymore.

Those who fall down into evil will have eternal death and bondage. Christ Himself tells us what will happen to the wicked that die impenitent:

And the unprofitable servant cast out into the exterior darkness.

There shall be weeping and gnashing of teeth. And when the Son of man shall come in his majesty, and all the angels with Him, then shall He sit upon the seat of his majesty. And all nations shall be gathered together before Him, and He shall separate them one from another, as the shepherd separates the sheep from the goats. And He shall set the sheep on His right hand, but the goats on His left. Then shall the King say to them that shall be on His right hand, "Come, you blessed of my Father, possess the kingdom prepared for you from the foundation of the world." (Mt 25:30–34)

Then he shall say to them also that shall be on his left hand, "Depart from me, you cursed, into everlasting fire which was prepared for the devil and his angels. For I was hungry, and you gave me not to eat; I was thirsty, and you gave me not to drink; I was a stranger, and you took me not in; naked, and you covered me not; sick and in prison, and you did not visit me."

Then they also shall answer him, saying, "Lord, when did we see You hungry, or thirsty, or a stranger, or naked, or sick, or in prison, and did not minister to thee?" Then He shall answer them, saying, "Amen I say to you, as long as you did it not to one of these least, neither did you do it to me." And these shall go into everlasting punishment, but the just, into life everlasting. (Mt 25:31–46)

It is better, Jesus says, to enter lame into everlasting life than having two feet and being cast into the hell of unquenchable fire "where the worm dies not, and the fire is not extinguished" (Mk 9: 44–45). The choice is ours. With our free will we can choose life, or choose death. In the book of Deuteronomy, the Lord promises that He will circumcise the hearts of His people that they may love God with their entire hearts and souls that they may live (De 30:6). He tells us that His Word is very near to us, in our mouths and hearts that we may do it (De 30:14).

> Consider that I have set before you this day life and good, and on the other hand death and evil. Love the Lord your God, and walk in His ways, and keep His commandments and ceremonies and judgments, and you may live, and He may multiply you, and bless you in the land, which you shall go in to possess. (De 30: 15–16)
>
> I call heaven and earth to witness this day, that I have set before you life and death, blessing and cursing. Choose therefore life that both you and your seed may live. (De 30:19)

If we do not choose life, we will be condemned to eternal death at the instant our souls separate from our bodies, as we leave this world and face the particular judgment each of us must face alone. Jesus will be our judge and one cannot appeal his judgment. However, if we choose life, Jesus will be to us more of a friend than judge, when we appear before Him.

In his book, *Life Everlasting*, the eminent Dominican scholar Father Reginald Garrigou-Lagrange, O.P. (1877–1964) describes the state of the soul that has been separated from the body by death. Although the separated soul no longer has sense operations, it does retain its sensitive faculties and its purely spiritual faculties—the intellect and the will and the habits that are located in these faculties. Interestingly, this author assures us that separated souls know each other (Garrigou-Lagrange 89).

The soul who is lost, now deprived of the things of sense that it enjoyed before it was separated from its body, becomes very painfully aware of the exceedingly great abyss of emptiness that is within, that only God can fill. When it reaches out for God, it is too late. Filled with despair, the damned soul realizes that it will never possess God and it becomes filled with hatred. "In hell," Garrigou-Lagrange affirms, "there is no love, only envy and isolation" (124). "The lost soul does not live. It is not dead. It dies without cessation, because it is forever away from God, the author of life" (124).

Heaven means the place and especially the condition of supreme beatitude (205). In heaven the blessed behold the beatific vision—the vision of God. The first and essential object is God Himself. The secondary object is creatures known in God" (227). Moreover, every saint in heaven knows all the others and especially those whom "he has known and loved on earth" (229).

In the book of Revelation, God promises us that there will be a new heaven and a new earth. Our bodies will be resurrected and glorified, never more to die.

The Venerable Luis de Granada, O.P. in his book *The Sinner's Guide* writes beautifully of heaven. This work has been a favorite book of a number of saints who treasured it—St. John of the Cross, St. Francis de Sales, St. Charles Borromeo, St. Vincent de Paul, St. Rose of Lima and St Teresa of Avila who stated that this book converted over a million souls in her time. Here is what Blessed Luis says about heaven:

> If your heart craves joy, raise it to the contemplation of that Good which contains in Itself all joys. If you are in love with this created life, consider the eternal life, which awaits you, above. If the beauty of creatures attracts you, live that you may one day possess the Source of all beauty, in whom are life, and strength, and glory, and immortality, and the fullness of all our desires. If you find happiness in friendship and the society of generous hearts, consider the noble beings with whom you will be united by the tenderest ties for all eternity. If your ambition seeks wealth and honors, make the treasures and the glory of Heaven the end of all your efforts. Finally, if you desire freedom from all evil and rest from all labor, in Heaven alone can your desires be gratified. (Ch 9)

Also speaking of the joys of heaven, Blessed Henry Suso tells us in *A Little Book of Eternal Wisdom*, that when we get to heaven that "the greatest stranger to thee of all its countless hosts will love thee more ardently and faithfully than any father or mother ever loved the child of their bosom in this scene of time" (Ch XII).

Describing the ninth heaven, Suso writes that it is "incalculably more than a hundred thousand times larger that the entire earth." He also writes of another heaven, Coelum Empyreum, the fiery heaven, so called because of its "transparent brightness." This is where the heavenly hosts dwell and God's children rejoice.

Suso describes the rewards of heaven as being of two kinds—accidental and essential.

> Accidental reward consists in such articular delight as souls obtain by particular and meritorious works wherewith they have conquered here below, even as the souls of great doctors, steadfast martyrs, and pure virgins. But essential reward consists in the contemplative union of the soul with the pure Divinity,

for rest she never can till she be borne above all her powers and capacities, and introduced to the natural entity of the Persons, and to the clear vision of their real essence. (Ch XII)

One of the most exciting concepts about heaven is expressed by St. Gregory of Nyssa (ca 330–ca 385). His mother was the daughter of a martyr, he and two of his brothers, Basil, known as St. Basil the Great and Peter of Sebaste, also a saint, became bishops. Their sister is St. Macrina. St. Gregory expresses his belief in the Doctrine of Infinite Growth in one of his sermons. In commenting on Paul's statement in Philippians 3:13, "But forgetting the things that are behind, I stretch forth to those that are before," he has the following remarks:

Yet even after listening in secret to the mysteries of heaven, Paul does not let the graces he has obtained become the limit of his desires, but he continues to go on and on, never ceasing his ascent. Thus he teaches us, I think, that in our constant participation in the blessed nature of the Good, the graces that we receive at every point are indeed great, but the path that lies beyond our immediate grasp is infinite. This will constantly happen to those who share in the divine Goodness, and they will always enjoy a greater and greater participation in grace throughout all eternity.

Thus though the new grace we may obtain is greater than what we had before, it does not put a limit on our final goal; rather, for those who are risen in perfection the limit of the good that is attained becomes the beginning of the discovery of higher goals. (211–213)

When we contemplate eternal life we must keep in mind that Christ has promised to raise from the grave all those who eat His Body and drink His Blood. We will not be disembodied spirits after our resurrection. Jesus tells us that He is the resurrection and the Life. The encounters of the Risen Christ by the Apostles and the five hundred others who saw Him all at one time help build our faith in the resurrection of us all who are in Christ. The *Catechism of the Catholic Church* teaches that we will rise from the dead in spiritual bodies that are like the body of the Risen Christ (999). Quoting St. Irenaeus (ca 120–ca 200), Bishop of Lyons, the *Catechism* explains that "our bodies which partake of the Eucharist, are no longer corruptible, but possess the hope of resurrection" (1000).

The resurrected saints will live forever with Christ in heaven. The *Catechism* explains, "To live in heaven is 'to be with Christ.' The elect live 'in Christ,' but they retain, or rather find, their true identity, their own name" (1025). Finally the *Catechism* concludes "In the glory of heaven, the blessed continue joyfully to fulfill God's will in relation to other men and to all creation. Already they reign with Christ; with Him 'they shall reign forever and ever'" (1029).

In conclusion, let us consider the wonderful promises that the Word of God gives us in the book of Revelation, if we remain faithful and true to Christ. If we overcome the world, the flesh, and the devil, the Lord will give us "to eat of the tree of life" (Rev 3: 7). He will give us "hidden manna" and a "white counter, and in the counter, a new name written," which no one knows except the one who receives it (Rev 2: 17). The morning star will He give to us (Rev 2: 28). Anyone who overcomes will be made "a pillar in the temple of My God, and he shall go out no more, and I will write upon him the name of My God, and the name of the city of My God, the new Jerusalem which comes down out of heaven from My God, and My new name (Rev 3: 12), To anyone who overcomes, Christ promises to let him sit with Him in His throne (3:21). We shall be a kingdom and priests and we shall reign on the earth (5: 10). There shall be a new heaven and a new earth (21: 1). God will dwell with us and we shall be His people. "And God shall wipe away all tears from their eyes: and death shall be no more, nor mourning, nor crying, nor sorrow shall be any more, for the former things are passed away" (21: 4). If anyone thirsts, God will give him of the "fountain of the water of life, freely" (21: 6).

In describing the heavenly city, the Holy Scripture says that there is no temple there for God Himself is its temple. Thee is no sun, nor moon, because the glory of God enlightens it (21: 22–23). "And the nations shall walk in the light of it, and the kings of the earth shall bring their glory and honor into it" (21: 24). "And there shall be no curse any more; but the throne of God and of the Lamb shall be in it, and His servants shall serve him. And they shall see His face: and His name shall be on their foreheads.

The Lord promises:

> Behold, I come quickly; and My reward is with Me, to render to every man according to his works. I am Alpha and Omega, the first and the last, the beginning and the end. Blessed are they that wash their robes in the blood of the Lamb, that they may have a right to the tree of life, and may enter in by the gates into the city. I, Jesus, have sent My angel, to testify to you these things in the churches. I am the root and stock of David, the bright and morning star. And the spirit and the bride say: Come. And he that hears, let him say: Come. And he that thirsts, let him come; and he that will, let him take the water of life, freely. (Rev 22: 16–17)

"Lord Jesus, we praise you for your great glory. We thank you, Heavenly Father, that it has pleased you to give us the kingdom. Holy Spirit, guide us safely through the perils of this world that we may come to the heavenly city and receive all the things the Father has planned for us. The magnificence of it all overwhelms us. With St. John the writer of the book of Revelation we say, "Maranatha! Come quickly, Lord Jesus!"

Notes

1. All Bible quotations and citations are from the Douay-Rheims version that is in the public domain. We have replaced archaic verb forms and pronouns with ones corresponding to modern usage. The Douay-Rheims can be found at http://www.gutenberg.org/

2. To anyone who wants to know more about New Age from a Catholic perspective, we recommend the study made by the Pontifical Council for Culture and the Pontifical Council for Interreligious dialogue, "Jesus Christ the Bearer of the Water of Life: A Christian reflection on the "New Age."

Works Cited

Albert the Great. *Quaestiones super de animalibus.* XV q. 11.

American Heritage Dictionary. Boston: Houghton Mifflin, 1980.

Aquinas, Thomas. *Summa Theologica.* II/II q. 49 a. 4.

Aristotle, "On the Generation of Animals."2, 3.

Augustine. *De catechizandis rudibus.* 4, 8: PL 40.

_____. *De genesi ad litteram.* 9, 5–9.

Bonaventure *The Soul's Journey into God. The Tree of Life. The Life of St Francis.* Paulist Press: Mahwah, NJ, 1978.

Cassian, John. *Conferences.* http://www.ewtn.com/library/PATRISTC/PII11-10.TXT.

_____. *Institutes.* http://www.osb.org/lectio/cassian/inst/.

Catechism of the Catholic Church. Liberaia Editrice: Vatican, 1994.

Chrysostom, John. "Homily on 2 Cor. 27." 3–4: PG 61, 588.

Cyprian, Thascius. "On Jealousy and Envy." http://www.ccel.org/fathers2/ANF-05/anf05120.htm.

_____. "On The Lord's Prayer" IV. http://www.ocf.org

First Vatican Council. "God Creator of All Things." http://www.ewtn.com/library/COUNCILS/V1.HTM.

Flannery, Austin. OP Ed. *The Conciliar and Post Conciliar Documents. Vatican Council II.* Boston: Daughters of St. Paul, 1988.

Francis de Sales. *Introduction to the Devout Life.* http://www.ccel.org/ccel/desales/devout_life.html.

Gregory of Nyssa. *From Glory to Glory.* Scribners: New York, 1961.

Hermas, *The Shepherd* in *The Fathers of the Church, The Apostolic Fathers.* Trans. Joseph Marique S.J, Ph.D. Catholic Univ Press: Washington, 1962.

Hogan, Richard. "An Introduction to John Paul II's Theology of the Body." http://www.nfpoutreach.org.

Pontifical Council for Culture and Pontifical Council for Interreligious Dialogue. "Jesus Christ the Bearer of the water of life." http://www.vatican.va/roman_curia/pontifical_councils/interelg/documents/rc_pc_interelg_doc_20030203_councils/interelg/documents/rc_pc_interelg_doc_20030203_new-age.

.John Paul II. *Crossing the Threshold of Hope.* Knopf: Canada, 1994.

_____. *John Paul II. Evangelium Vitae.* vatican.va.edocs/ENG)141/_PG>HTM.

_____. John Paul II. Qtd by Archbishop Norberto Rivera Carrera. in "A Call to Vigilance: Pastoral-Instruction on the New Age." http://www.ourladyswarriors.org/dissent/newage1.htm.

Josephus, Flavius. *Antiquities.* http://www.ccel.org/j/josephus/JOSEPHUS.HTM.

Leo III. *Libertas*
http://www.vatican.va/holy_father/leo_xiii/encyclicals/documents/hf_l-xiiienc_20061888 __ libertas_en.html.

Luis de Granada. *The Sinner's Guide.* http://www.ewtn.com/library/SPIRIT/granada.htm.

Merkle, Clare McGrath, O.C.D.S. "In the Arms of Jesus and Mary." http://www.crossveil.org/page6.html.

Pacwa, Mitch SJ. "The Enneagram: Spirituality it is Not." http://www,.petersnet.net/research/retrieve_full.cfm? RecNum=2622.

Rodriguez, Alphonsus. Qtd. In Poulain, Auguste, SJ. *The Graces of Interior Prayer*. Celtic Cross Books: Westminster, VT, 1949. 268–269.

Suso, Henry. *A Little Book of Eternal Wisdom*. http://www.ccel.org/s/suso/wisdom/wisdom.htm

Tanquerey, Adolphe. *The Spiritual Life*. Desclee: Paris, 1930.

Tertullian. "Of Patience" http://newadvent.org/fathers/0325.htm.

About the Authors

Ricardo C. Castellanos, LST

Born in Camaguey, Cuba in 1945, Rev. Ricardo Castellanos came to the United States in 1961. He received a B. A. degree in philosophy from the Granada Dominican College in Granada, Spain. From the Gregorian University in Rome, he received his LST degree in theology and was ordained May 17, 1970 in St. Peter's Basilica in Rome by Pope Paul VI. He has lectured extensively on motivational topics on television and radio throughout the United States, Europe, South America, and in an outreach ministry in the Middle East and Japan. He is the author of countless motivational audio and video materials in both Spanish and English, including *Attacks on the Family*, *Ten Steps to Refresh Your Marriage*, *The Family*, *Anger and Pardon*, *Interior Healing*, *Steps in Christian Family Living*, *El Camino del Gozo*, *No tengas miedo*, *Pasos para Sana Nuestra Imagen*, *Los Fenómenos del Occultismo*, and *Los Angeles y Los Demonios*, among countless others. He is also coauthor with Allienne Becker of *All You Need Is Love: The Way of Joy*, Writers Club Press, 2003. To learn more about these materials visit the website www.beckerinprint.com.

Allienne R. Becker, Ph.D.

Dr. Allienne R. Becker has a B. A. degree from Duke University, two M. A. degrees from West Virginia University, and a Ph.D. from the Pennsylvania State University. She is an emerita of the State System of Higher Education for the Commonwealth of Pennsylvania, having taught at Lock Haven University for twenty-seven years, and is the author of several academic books published by Greenwood Press. Her interest in religion and hagiography led her to publishing *I, Paul...: The Life of the Apostle to the Gentiles,* Writers Club Press, 2001 and *Eagle in Flight: the Life of Athanasius, the Apostle of the Trinity,* Writers Club Press, 2002. She is also coauthor with Ricardo Castellanos of *All You Need Is Love: The Way of Joy,* Writers Club Press, 2003. For more information about her books see www.beckerinprint.com.

Be Free!: The Gift of Freedom explains how to find freedom and transform our lives making us people of great joy and happiness, by showing how to overcome fear, anger, guilt, deception, and other things that keep us from being free. The book describes the peace and contentment that flow from those who have attained freedom and liberty.

0-595-30539-3